# EDWARD SPENCER

# NARRATIVE CONTROL: Media Bias, Censorship & Elections 2024

*The Fight for Truth Amidst Media Narratives and Election Propaganda*

CENTURION
PRESS

"Whoever controls the media, controls
the mind."
— Jim Morrison

# Contents

# Preface

The idea for this book was born out of my academic journey and my passion for uncovering the truth amidst political narratives. It began as a personal exploration during my master's and doctoral research, delving into the complex interplay between media bias, censorship, and political influence. The original concepts evolved as I witnessed firsthand the challenges of maintaining narrative control in the face of powerful propaganda during election cycles.

This book aims to shed light on the intricate mechanisms through which media narratives are shaped, the biases that are often hidden from public view, and the impact these have on the democratic process. In researching for this book, I explored how misinformation, censorship, and agenda-driven reporting influence public perception and ultimately, elections.

The fight for truth has never been more critical, and this book serves as both an analysis and a call to action. It is intended for anyone interested in understanding the role of media in shaping political realities, especially during crucial moments like elections.

I would like to express my deepest gratitude to my mentors who have supported me throughout this journey, as well as to the journalists, researchers, and activists whose work has been instrumental in shaping the discussions presented here.

I hope this book will inspire readers to question the information they consume, recognize biases, and become more informed participants in the fight for an open and truthful media landscape.

# Introduction

In the months leading up to the 2024 U.S. election, or any election in the world nowadays, for that matter, the battle for truth isn't fought in the voting booths or in debates; it is fought on our screens, in our feeds, and in our minds. The noise is deafening—a relentless cascade of headlines, viral tweets, and breaking news alerts, each one vying for our attention, each claiming to present the "real story." It is a time when narratives blur into propaganda, and even the most discerning citizens struggle to navigate a sea of half-truths, spin, and outright lies.

The political landscape is more fragmented than ever. On one side, we have media outlets that lean heavily into one ideology, reinforcing biases and catering to an audience that craves validation rather than information. On the other side, we find media organizations that claim neutrality, yet subtly, or sometimes not-so-subtly, promote a narrative that aligns with their preferred political outcomes. In the midst of this, voters are left bewildered, unsure of where to find the truth, or whether such a thing even exists anymore. The media, once seen as the fourth estate, a watchdog for democracy, has become an arena of warring factions—each pushing an agenda, each contributing to the erosion of trust in journalism itself.

The erosion of journalistic integrity is not a one-sided issue. Both left-leaning and right-leaning media outlets have abandoned their roles as independent journalists, becoming activists for their respective causes. Headlines are crafted not necessarily to inform but to provoke—to generate clicks, shares, and ultimately, revenue. In this environment, the truth is not only a casualty; it is often the last thing on anyone's mind. Sensationalism sells, and outrage drives engagement, leaving little room for balanced reporting or objective analysis.

As we approach the final weeks of the 2024 election, the stakes have never been higher. The power of media bias, censorship, and misinformation is palpable, shaping the narrative and swaying public opinion in ways that are often invisible to the average citizen. Algorithms designed by tech companies amplify emotionally charged content, creating echo chambers where users are fed information that aligns with their existing beliefs. This creates a cycle of reinforcement, where misinformation is not only spread but becomes deeply entrenched. It is no longer enough to simply be informed; one must actively seek out credible sources, fact-check claims, and remain vigilant against manipulation.

Candidates and their campaigns are acutely aware of the power of perception, using every tool at their disposal to craft messages that resonate. Carefully curated ads, targeted social media campaigns, and even selective appearances on sympathetic media channels are all part of the strategy to control the narrative. The truth often becomes a casualty in the race for influence. Each side accuses the other of deception, while both engage in the same tactics—twisting facts, omitting inconvenient truths, and amplifying stories that serve their interests.

This book, "Narrative Control: Media Bias, Censorship, and Election 2024," aims to dissect the forces that shape the information landscape during this pivotal election. It will explore how media manipulation, censorship, and deliberate misinformation influence outcomes and widen the chasms of distrust and division within the country. We will examine key moments when truth is twisted, platforms that fail in their duty, and the very real consequences that come from a battle waged not with bullets or ballots, but with stories—crafted, curated, and controlled.

To understand the magnitude of this issue, we must look beyond individual headlines or viral posts. We must examine the infrastructure that allows misinformation to flourish—the algorithms, the profit-driven motives of media corporations, and the ideological divides that have turned news into a weapon. We will explore how the very platforms designed to connect us have instead deepened divisions, and how the pursuit of profit has compromised the role of the press as a defender of democracy.

As we delve into the mechanics of media influence and its impact on the democratic process, we must confront a vital question: In an era where information is power, how do we reclaim the truth? With the 2024 election just around the corner, understanding this battle for narrative control is not just an exercise in analysis—it is a necessary step toward safeguarding the future of democracy. The fight for truth is ongoing, and the outcome will determine not only who wins an election but the kind of society we wish to build. Will we allow misinformation to dictate our choices, or will we demand better—from our media, our leaders, and ourselves?

# 1

# Key Terms & Concepts

To understand the rise and impact of misinformation in today's society, it is essential to establish a foundational understanding of the key terms and concepts that will be used throughout this book. Terms such as misinformation, disinformation, fake news, echo chambers, filter bubbles, and voter suppression are often used in discussions about the modern information landscape, yet they are frequently misunderstood or conflated.

This chapter aims to provide clear definitions and real-world examples of these concepts to ensure that readers are equipped with the necessary knowledge to comprehend the broader discussions that follow. By establishing a shared understanding of these key terms, we can better explore how misinformation spreads, the factors that contribute to its proliferation, and its impact on society.

Throughout this chapter, we will define each term in detail, provide context on how it fits into the modern information ecosystem, and illustrate its effects with examples. This approach will lay the groundwork for analyzing the evolution of misinformation, the role of technology, and the challenges faced by democracies in an age of information overload.

The goal is not only to define these terms but also to understand how they interact with each other in the digital age. The interplay between misinformation, technology, and human psychology has created a complex web that influences public perception, shapes political discourse, and impacts daily decision-making. As we move through the subsequent chapters, these key concepts will serve as building blocks for a more nuanced understanding of the challenges posed by misinformation in today's world.

## 1.1 Misinformation

**Misinformation** refers to false or misleading information that is spread without malicious intent. It often arises from misunderstandings, misinterpretations, or the casual sharing of unchecked information. According to the Merriam-Webster Dictionary, misinformation is defined as "incorrect or misleading information" (Merriam-Webster, n.d.). Importantly, misinformation is not necessarily spread with the purpose of causing harm; rather, it can be the result of human error, incomplete understanding, or even simple rumors. Unlike disinformation, misinformation does not have an underlying intent to deceive, which makes it particularly challenging to address, as individuals may not even be aware that they are spreading false information.

***Example of Misinformation:***
**COVID-19 Misinformation:** During the COVID-19 pandemic,

misinformation about potential cures, the origins of the virus, and the effects of vaccines spread rapidly across social media. One common piece of misinformation claimed that drinking bleach could cure COVID-19. Despite health authorities like the World Health Organization (WHO) and the Centers for Disease Control and Prevention (CDC) debunking this claim, it still led to people being hospitalized for attempting to ingest harmful substances. Source: World Health Organization. (2020). Coronavirus disease (COVID-19) advice for the public: Mythbusters. Retrieved from https://www.who.int/emergencies/diseases/novel-coronavirus-2019/advice-for-public/myth-busters

## 1.2 Disinformation

**Disinformation** is characterized by its intentionality. The Cambridge Dictionary defines disinformation as "false information spread in order to deceive people" (Cambridge Dictionary, n.d.). Unlike misinformation, disinformation is deliberate and is typically used as a tool for manipulation. Governments, political actors, and other entities often use disinformation to influence public opinion, control narratives, or destabilize adversaries. It is a strategic effort designed to mislead people, often to serve political, economic, or ideological goals. Disinformation campaigns can be highly organized, using advanced technology, coordinated networks, and psychological tactics to target specific audiences and achieve desired outcomes.

***Example of Disinformation:***
In 2013, during the Boston Marathon bombing, deliberate dis-

information spread on social media, falsely accusing innocent individuals of being involved in the attack. One notable instance was the spread of manipulated images and claims that a specific college student, who had gone missing, was one of the suspects. This disinformation was intentionally spread by some users to disrupt the investigation and gain attention, despite there being no evidence linking the individual to the incident. This spread of false information not only hindered the investigation but also caused distress for the family of the falsely accused individual. **Source**: Starbird, K., Maddock, J., Orand, M., Achterman, P., & Mason, R. M. (2014). Rumors, False Flags, and Digital Vigilantes: Misinformation on X After the 2013 Boston Marathon Bombing. Retrieved from https://www.researchgate.net/publication/26 6629432_Rumors_False_Flags_and_Digital_Vigilantes_M isinformation_on_X_After_the_2013_Boston_Marathon_ Bombing

## 1.3 Malinformation

**Malinformation** refers to information that is based on factual content but is used with the intent to cause harm by placing it in a misleading context. Unlike misinformation, which is false but spread without intent to deceive, and disinformation, which is false and spread with deliberate intent to deceive, malinformation involves *true information* that is manipulated to damage reputations or mislead in harmful ways.

An example of malinformation is "revenge porn", where private photos are shared publicly with malicious intent, changing the context from private to public and causing harm. Another instance is providing factual information, such as the timing or location of an event, but altering the context to mislead people. This type of content aims to cause harm by using truthful information in a damaging or misleading way. Retrieved from: https://en.wikipedia.org/wiki/Malinformation

## 1.4 Conspiracy Theories

**Conspiracy theories** are narratives that suggest hidden plots by powerful groups, often involving secrecy and deception, usually without substantial evidence to support them. They are built around the belief that powerful individuals or organizations are orchestrating secretive actions for malevolent purposes. According to the Cambridge Dictionary, a conspiracy theory is defined as "a belief that an event or situation is the result of a secret plan made by powerful people" (Cambridge Dictionary, n.d.). Conspiracy theories can spread misinformation by promoting false or misleading claims, and they are often shared without verification of their accuracy.

Conspiracy theories can fall under the category of **misinformation** or **disinformation**, depending on the circumstances and intent. They are misinformation when they involve false claims that are spread by individuals who believe them to be true, without any malicious intent. On the other hand, they can be considered disinformation when they are deliberately fabricated or spread with the intent to deceive or manipulate public opinion. For example, conspiracy theories about political figures can be spread to influence elections, sway public sentiment, or undermine trust in institutions.

The nature of conspiracy theories makes them particularly challenging to address, as they often rely on cherry-picked facts, coincidences, and skepticism of official accounts. While some conspiracy theories may contain elements of truth, many are ultimately based on flawed logic or lack substantial evidence, contributing to the overall spread of misinformation in society. They can erode trust in institutions, incite fear, and, in some cases, lead to real-world consequences, such as violence or public harm.

***Example of a Conspiracy Theory:***

**Pizzagate Conspiracy**: In 2016, a piece of misinformation known as "Pizzagate" spread widely across social media platforms, claiming that a child trafficking ring involving high-profile politicians was being operated out of a pizzeria in Washington, D.C. Despite there being no evidence to support these claims, the misinformation led to real-world consequences, including a man entering the restaurant with a firearm, believing he was rescuing victims. Source: BBC News. (2016). Pizzagate: The fake story that shows how conspiracy theories spread. Retrieved from https://www.bbc.com/news/blogs-trending-38156985

## 1.5 Fake News

**Fake news** is another term that has gained considerable attention in recent years, though it is somewhat ambiguous. It generally refers to news stories that are fabricated and presented as legitimate journalism, with the intent to mislead.

The Oxford English Dictionary defines fake news as "false, often sensational, information disseminated under the guise of news reporting" (Oxford English Dictionary, n.d.). However, the term is not a recent invention; it has existed long before the internet and social media. In the past, before the internet, fake news was spread through traditional forms of the media in order to influence and control public opinion, but people were often unaware of its existence and impact.

***Example of Fake News:***

In the USA during the 1800s, sensationalized and fabricated stories were commonly used in newspapers, often referred to as "yellow journalism," to influence public opinion on political and social issues. Internationally, during World War II, propaganda containing fake news was distributed by various countries to sway public sentiment and demoralize enemy populations. Fake news can encompass both misinformation and disinformation, depending on the intent behind its creation and dissemination. The rise of social media has facilitated the spread of fake news, as individuals are often unable to discern between credible news sources and fabricated stories designed to provoke an emotional reaction or generate clicks for financial gain.

## 1.6 Propaganda

**Propaganda** is defined by the Oxford Learner's Dictionary as "information, especially of a biased or misleading nature, used to promote a political cause or point of view" (Oxford Learner's Dictionary, n.d.). Propaganda has been used throughout history as a tool for influencing public opinion, often by presenting one-sided or distorted information. Governments and political organizations have traditionally used propaganda to control narratives, especially during times of conflict or political upheaval. Unlike misinformation, which may be spread without intent, propaganda is always intentional and seeks to influence people's beliefs or behaviors to support a particular agenda.

***Example of Propaganda:***

During **World War II**, propaganda was extensively used by many countries to influence public opinion and boost support for the war effort. For instance, the United States produced posters, films, and radio broadcasts depicting enemy nations in a negative light to build national unity and justify the war. These materials often exaggerated or fabricated information to generate fear and foster a sense of patriotism, ensuring that the general public remained committed to the war effort.

# 1.7 Hoax

A **hoax** is an act intended to deceive or trick people into believing something false. According to Merriam-Webster, a hoax is "an act intended to trick or dupe" (Merriam-Webster, n.d.). Hoaxes can take many forms, from false scientific claims to fabricated news stories, and are often spread for entertainment, financial gain, or to create confusion. Hoaxes can be particularly damaging when they involve serious matters, such as public health or safety, as they can lead to widespread fear or dangerous behavior.

***Example of a Political Hoax:***

The **Russian collusion hoax** is often cited as an example of a politically charged event where claims were made that the Trump campaign colluded with Russian officials to influence the outcome of the 2016 U.S. presidential election. While the investigation by Special Counsel Robert Mueller found that Russia did attempt to interfere with the election, no conclusive evidence was found to establish that the Trump campaign conspired or coordinated with the Russian government. Despite this, the narrative of collusion was widely circulated in the media, causing significant political turmoil and influencing public perception for years. The **Mueller Report** is an objective legal document, and its language is careful not to present definitive statements about motives or to characterize the investigation as a "hoax." The conclusion about insufficient evidence is interpreted by some as evidence that the collusion claims were politically motivated, which is where the "hoax" term originates in public discourse.

***Example of a Media-driven Hoax:***

The **"Duke Lacrosse Case" hoax** is an example of a media-driven hoax in the United States. In 2006, members of the Duke University men's lacrosse team were accused of sexually assaulting an exotic dancer hired to perform at a party. The accusations received extensive media coverage, and many outlets presented the story as an example of privilege and misconduct. However, after a lengthy investigation, it was determined that the allegations were false, and all charges against the players were dropped. The prosecutor in the case, Mike Nifong, was later disbarred for unethical conduct, including withholding evidence that exonerated the accused players. This incident is often cited as an example of how media coverage can contribute to the spread of false narratives before the facts are fully established. **Source**: Taylor, S., & Johnson, K. (2007). *Until Proven Innocent: Political Correctness and the Shameful Injustices of the Duke Lacrosse Rape Case*. Thomas Dunne Books. Retrieved from https://search.lib.uiowa.edu/primo-explore/fulldisplay/01IOWA_ALMA21409559370002771/01IOWA

## 1.8 Infodemic

**Infodemic** is a term coined by the World Health Organization (WHO) to describe an overabundance of information—some accurate and some not—that makes it difficult for people to find trustworthy sources and reliable guidance (World Health Organization, n.d.).

***Example of an Infodemic:***
The COVID-19 pandemic is a prime example of an infodemic, as misinformation about the virus, treatments, and vaccines spread widely, contributing to public confusion and hindering effective responses. The infodemic was a key factor in the challenges faced by health authorities around the world, as misinformation competed with accurate information, often leading to public distrust in vaccines, health measures, and institutions. During the early months of the pandemic, social media platforms were flooded with misinformation and disinformation, ranging from false claims about the virus's origins to unverified home remedies and conspiracy theories. For instance, false claims about the virus being caused by 5G

networks led to vandalism of cell towers in several countries. The overwhelming amount of information, much of which was misleading, caused confusion and contributed to public mistrust of health authorities and recommended preventive measures. **Source**: World Health Organization. (2020). *Managing the COVID-19 infodemic: Promoting healthy behaviors and mitigating the harm from misinformation and disinformation.* Retrieved from https://www.who.int/news/item/23-09-2020-managing-the-covid-19-infodemic-promoting-healthy-behaviours-and-mitigating-the-harm-from-misinformation-and-disinformation

## 1.9 Echo Chamber

An **echo chamber** is an environment in which a person encounters only beliefs or opinions that coincide with their own, thus reinforcing their existing views. The Oxford Learner's Dictionary defines an echo chamber as an environment where alternative ideas are not considered (Oxford Learner's Dictionary, n.d.). Social media platforms, through their algorithms, often create echo chambers by showing users content that aligns with their preferences, which can amplify misinformation. Echo chambers contribute to the polarization of society by creating isolated bubbles where individuals only receive information that confirms their biases, limiting the exchange of diverse perspectives.

***Example of an Echo Chamber:***
An example of an echo chamber is how social media al-

gorithms, such as those used by Facebook, can create personalized content feeds that predominantly show users posts and information that align with their existing beliefs and interests. During the 2020 U.S. presidential election, many users were shown political content that reinforced their own views, leading to further polarization. These algorithm-driven echo chambers made it difficult for individuals to be exposed to differing viewpoints, contributing to an environment where misinformation could thrive unchecked. **Source**: Tucker, J. A., Guess, A., Barbera, P., Vaccari, C., Siegel, A., Sanovich, S., Stukal, D., & Nyhan, B. (2018). *Social Media, Political Polarization, and Political Disinformation: A Review of the Scientific Literature.* Retrieved from https://papers.ssrn.com/sol3/papers.cfm?abstract_id=3144139

## 1.10 Filter Bubble

A **filter bubble** is closely related to the concept of an echo chamber. Cambridge Dictionary defines a filter bubble as a situation in which someone only sees news and information that supports their existing ideas because websites automatically decide what information to give them based on previous internet behavior (Cambridge Dictionary, n.d.). Filter bubbles limit exposure to diverse perspectives and contribute to the spread of misinformation by reinforcing pre-existing beliefs. Filter bubbles can make it difficult for individuals to access reliable, balanced information, as algorithms prioritize content that is likely to engage them, rather than challenge their views.

***Example of a Filter Bubble****:*

An example of a filter bubble is how Google's personalized search algorithm tailors search results to individual users based on their previous searches, location, and browsing history. This personalization can lead to users only seeing content that reinforces their existing viewpoints, without exposure to diverse perspectives or information that contradicts their beliefs. For instance, if a user frequently searches for content that supports a particular political ideology, they may primarily receive search results that confirm their views, effectively creating a filter bubble. This phenomenon can contribute to increased polarization and limit users' awareness of other perspectives. **Source**: Zuiderveen Borgesius, F. J., Trilling, D., Moeller, J., Bodó, B., de Vreese, C. H., & Helberger, N. (2016). *Should we worry about filter bubbles?* Internet Policy Review, 5(1). Retrieved from https://escholarship.org/content/qt8w7105jp/qt8w7105jp.pdf

## 1.11 Algorithm

To fully understand the rise of misinformation and its impact in the digital age, it is also important to define the term **algorithm**. Algorithms play a crucial role in shaping the information people see, particularly on social media platforms, and understanding their function is essential to comprehending how misinformation spreads and is amplified. Algorithms determine what content is prioritized, recommended, or hidden, based on user behavior and engagement metrics. As such, they are central to the mechanisms of echo chambers, filter bubbles, and the viral nature of misinformation.

An **algorithm** is defined by the Cambridge Dictionary as "a set of mathematical instructions or rules that, especially if given to a computer, will help to calculate an answer or solve a problem" (Cambridge Dictionary, n.d.). In the context of information technology, algorithms are used by social media platforms to determine what content is shown to users based on their past behavior, preferences, and engagement. The Merriam-Webster Dictionary defines an algorithm as "a procedure for solving a mathematical problem in a finite number of steps that frequently involves repetition of an operation" or more broadly as "a step-by-step procedure for solving a problem or accomplishing some end" (Merriam-Webster, n.d.).

Algorithms are instrumental in creating **filter bubbles** and **echo chambers**, as they curate content to match users' preferences, often reinforcing existing beliefs and limiting exposure to diverse viewpoints. This selective content delivery can contribute to the spread of misinformation, as users are more likely to see and engage with information that aligns with their interests and emotions, regardless of its accuracy. Understanding algorithms and their influence on information dissemination is therefore a critical component of addressing the challenges posed by misinformation in the digital age.

***Example of Algorithm:***

One common example of an algorithm is the **Google Search algorithm**. When a user types a query into the search bar, Google's algorithm processes the query and quickly analyzes billions of web pages to deliver the most relevant results. It considers various factors, such as keyword relevance, page quality, and user location, to rank and display the results.

This step-by-step process helps users find the information they are looking for in a matter of seconds, illustrating how algorithms can solve complex problems by following specific sets of rules. **Source**: Search Engine Journal. (2023). *What Are Search Algorithms & How Do They Work?*. Retrieved from https://www.searchenginejournal.com/search-engines/algorithms/

## 1.12 Astroturfing

**Astroturfing** is defined by Merriam-Webster as "organized activity that is intended to create a false impression of a spontaneous grassroots movement" (Merriam-Webster, n.d.). Astroturfing is a tactic often used in political campaigns or marketing efforts to make it appear as though there is widespread support for a particular cause or product when, in reality, it is a coordinated effort by a small group. The term "astroturfing" comes from "AstroTurf," a brand of synthetic grass, implying that what appears to be genuine grassroots support is, in fact, artificial. Astroturfing is problematic because it can manipulate public perception, making certain viewpoints seem more popular or legitimate than they actually are.

*Example of Astroturfing:*
An example of astroturfing occurred when a large company launched a public campaign to oppose proposed environmental regulations. The company created a fake grassroots organization that appeared to be made up of concerned citizens advocating against the regulations, arguing they would harm local

businesses and lead to job losses. In reality, the organization was funded and coordinated by the company itself, and its activities were designed to sway public opinion and policy in favor of the company's interests. This artificial support gave the impression of widespread opposition to the regulations, despite the true motivations being corporate profit. **Source**: Beder, S. (2019). *Public Relations' Role in Manufacturing Artificial Grass Roots Coalitions*. Retrieved from https://www.researchga te.net/publication/238304605_Public_Relations'_Role_in_ Manufacturing_Artificial_Grass_Roots_Coalitions

## 1.13 Gaslighting

**Gaslighting** is a form of psychological manipulation in which a person or group makes someone question their own reality or sanity. The Oxford English Dictionary defines gaslighting as "a form of psychological manipulation in which a person or group covertly sows seeds of doubt in a targeted individual or group, making them question their own memory, perception, or judgment" (Oxford English Dictionary, n.d.). Gaslighting can be used in the context of misinformation to make people doubt factual evidence and question their understanding of reality. This tactic is often employed in political discourse to discredit opponents, undermine trust in credible sources, or sow confusion among the public.

*Example of Gaslighting:*
   **Bipartisan Gaslighting in 2024**: During recent debates over the national crime rate, both major political parties have pre-

sented conflicting narratives, often ignoring data provided by nonpartisan sources. Politicians from one party have argued that crime has significantly decreased nationwide and that safety concerns are overblown, even though the **Federal Bureau of Investigation (FBI)** reported increases in violent crime in some urban areas.  Meanwhile, politicians from the other party have painted a picture of crime being "out of control" across the entire country, which is also not supported by the comprehensive data, as many cities have seen stable or declining crime rates.  By selectively using crime statistics to fit their narrative, both parties have contributed to public confusion regarding the actual state of public safety in the country. **Source**: Federal Bureau of Investigation. (2024). *Crime in the United States*. Retrieved from https://www.fbi.gov/how-we-can-help-you/more-fbi-services-and-information/ucr

## 1.14 Censorship

**Censorship** is defined by the Oxford English Dictionary as "the suppression or prohibition of any parts of books, films, news, etc. that are considered obscene, politically unacceptable, or a threat to security" (Oxford English Dictionary, n.d.).  In a broader sense, censorship refers to the deliberate suppression or restriction of information, ideas, or expressions by governments, private institutions, or other controlling bodies to prevent the public from accessing certain content. The Cambridge Dictionary defines censorship as "the act of preventing parts of books, films, or news from being seen or read by the public because they are considered to be offensive or a political threat"

(Cambridge Dictionary, n.d.).

Censorship can take various forms, such as the restriction of media content, internet regulation, or the banning of books, with the intent of controlling public perception or preventing dissent. It is often used by governments or authorities to maintain control, protect national security, or limit the spread of certain ideas deemed harmful or controversial.

***Example of Censorship:***

**Government Censorship**: During the **Arab Spring** in 2011, several governments in the Middle East and North Africa implemented internet censorship to suppress information and prevent protests from gaining momentum. In countries like **Egypt** and **Tunisia**, authorities restricted access to social media platforms such as Facebook and X, which were being used by activists to organize demonstrations and share real-time updates. This form of censorship aimed to stifle the flow of information, prevent the spread of revolutionary ideas, and maintain control over the populace during a period of significant political upheaval. **Source**: Howard, P. N., & Hussain, M. M. (2013). *Democracy's Fourth Wave? Digital Media and the Arab Spring.* Oxford University Press. Retrieved from https://academic.oup.com/book/12228/chapter-abstract/161707586?redirectedFrom=fulltext

## 1.15 Fact-Checking

**Fact-checking** is the process of verifying information to determine its accuracy, often with the aim of preventing the spread of false or misleading content. According to the Cambridge Dictionary, fact-checking is defined as "the process of checking all the facts in a piece of writing, news article, speech, etc., to make sure that they are correct" (Cambridge Dictionary, n.d.). Fact-checkers are individuals or organizations that carry out this process, using evidence and reputable sources to assess the validity of claims made in public discourse.

The Merriam-Webster Dictionary defines a **fact-checker** as "a person who verifies the factual accuracy of an article before publication" (Merriam-Webster, n.d.). Fact-checkers play an essential role in journalism, where the accuracy of information is crucial for maintaining public trust. Fact-checking organizations, such as PolitiFact, Snopes, and FactCheck.org, have gained prominence in recent years, particularly in the context of misinformation and disinformation spread online.

Fact-checking has become an important part of the digital information ecosystem, particularly with the rise of misinformation on social media. Fact-checkers aim to provide the public with accurate information and counter false claims by evaluating statements made by public figures, news articles, and viral social media posts.

***Example of Fact-Checking:***

A well-known example of fact-checking occurred during the COVID-19 pandemic, when misinformation about vaccines spread widely online. Fact-checking organizations worked to verify claims about the effectiveness and safety of vaccines, often labeling false statements as "incorrect" or "misleading" on social media platforms. Facebook partnered with third-party fact-checkers to flag and reduce the spread of false information related to COVID-19. These fact-checks helped guide the public towards accurate information during a critical health crisis.

***Fact-Checking as a Form of Control:***

While fact-checking is often presented as an impartial effort to promote accuracy, critics argue that it can be used as a means for media companies and technology platforms to control speech and ideas. Because fact-checking organizations often operate in collaboration with major tech platforms like Facebook, X, and Google, concerns have been raised that fact-checking is subject to biases, reflecting the viewpoints of those who fund or partner with these efforts. This has led to accusations that fact-checking can be used to suppress certain perspectives while elevating others, effectively shaping public discourse in ways that align with the interests of powerful actors.

Fact-checkers may label content that questions the mainstream narrative on certain topics as "false" or "misleading," even when the claims are debatable or open to interpretation. This practice can limit the diversity of perspectives and restrict free expression, as content that does not align with the established viewpoints of fact-checking organizations or their partners may be downranked or removed entirely. The role of fact-checking as a tool for controlling speech raises important questions about who decides what is "true" and whether this concentration of power serves the public interest.

# 1.16 Voter suppression

**Voter Suppression**: Voter suppression refers to any effort or strategy used to discourage or prevent certain groups of people from voting, often by creating barriers to their ability to register or cast their ballots. According to Merriam-Webster, voter suppression is defined as "a strategy used to influence the outcome of an election by discouraging or preventing people from exercising the right to vote" (Merriam-Webster, n.d.). The Oxford English Dictionary also describes voter suppression as "the action of discouraging or preventing a person or group of people from voting, especially by using discriminatory practices or by imposing unnecessary obstacles to the voting process" (Oxford English Dictionary, n.d.).

Voter suppression can also occur indirectly through the use of misinformation and media manipulation, especially in the age of the internet and social media. Disinformation campaigns, discouraging voter participation, and micro-targeting with ads are just a few of the methods that can be used to influence people indirectly and suppress voter turnout.

***Examples of Voter Suppression:***

**Incorrect Voting Information Spread on Social Media**: In the **2018 U.S. midterm elections**, misinformation was spread on social media platforms, including incorrect information about voting dates and polling locations. This misinformation was not tied to a specific candidate or party but was aimed at causing confusion among voters. For example, false posts claimed that Democrats should vote on Wednesday while Republicans should vote on Tuesday, even though Election Day was the same for everyone. **Source**: American Progress. (2019). *Voter Suppression During the 2018 Midterm Elections.* Retrieved from https://www .americanprogress.org/article/voter-suppression-2018-midt erm-elections/

## 1.17 Election Interference

**Election interference** refers to any deliberate attempt by individuals, organizations, or foreign entities to disrupt, influence, or alter the outcome of an election. This interference can take many forms, including disinformation campaigns, cyberattacks, financial influence, or manipulating voter information. The goal of election interference is often to undermine democratic processes, create public distrust in the electoral system, or sway election outcomes in favor of a specific candidate or party.

The **Oxford English Dictionary** defines election interference as "the illicit involvement or disruption in a democratic electoral process by foreign or domestic actors, typically aiming to influence or subvert the result" (Oxford English Dictionary, n.d.).

*Examples of Election Interference:*

**U.S. Presidential Election 2016**: In the 2016 U.S. election, Russian interference was widely reported. According to investigations by U.S. intelligence agencies, Russian actors used disinformation campaigns on social media platforms like Facebook and X to polarize the electorate and influence public perception. They created fake accounts and groups to spread misinformation, promote divisive content, and support certain candidates while attacking others. This interference aimed to undermine faith in U.S. democratic institutions.

This phenomenon is not limited to a single country or election; it has become a **worldwide issue** as countries like **Russia, China, and Iran** increasingly use the internet to influence elections in Western democracies. These countries have employed tactics such as disinformation campaigns, hacking attempts, and the use of fake social media accounts to shape public perception and create distrust in democratic institutions. In recent years, intelligence agencies have identified multiple attempts by foreign actors to manipulate electoral outcomes in the **U.S., the United Kingdom, Germany, France**, and other Western nations.

For instance, in addition to Russia's well-documented efforts, **China** has also been reported to use influence campaigns to promote narratives favorable to its interests, especially targeting Western countries. **Iran** has engaged in spreading disinformation to exacerbate social tensions, focusing on polarizing issues like racial and religious differences. These campaigns are often carried out through sophisticated networks of fake accounts and bots, aimed at amplifying divisive content and sowing discord among the public. More about these international disinformation campaigns will be discussed in **Chapter 2**. Retrieved from https://www.nytimes.com/2024/09/04/business/media/iran-disinformation-us-presidential-race.html

# 1.18 Conclusion

In this chapter, we have established the foundational terms and concepts necessary to navigate the complex landscape of misinformation. Understanding these definitions is crucial for the discussions that follow, as each concept plays a role in how information is created, shared, and interpreted in today's digital world. The distinctions between misinformation, disinformation, fake news, and the factors that amplify their spread—such as echo chambers and filter bubbles—form the basis of our analysis of the rise and impact of false information.

While the book uses "misinformation" as a general term, it encompasses a variety of manipulative information strategies, including those that are intentional, malicious, or part of a larger narrative. By simplifying these different types of information manipulation under the umbrella of "misinformation," we aim to provide a cohesive understanding of the broader challenges associated with false information in our digital age.

To better capture the wide spectrum of phenomena discussed in this book, we also use the term "manipulated information" or "information manipulation." This broader term captures a wider range of phenomena, including:

- **Misinformation** (unintentionally false information)
- **Disinformation** (deliberately false information with intent to deceive)
- **Malinformation** (accurate information used maliciously to cause harm)
- **Propaganda** (information designed to influence public perception for political or ideological purposes)

- **False Narratives** (constructed stories that misrepresent events, often using selective truths and misinformation)

**"Manipulated information"** or **"information manipulation"** allows us to cover all these types without being restricted to just unintentional inaccuracies or deliberate falsehoods. This broader term captures the intent to influence, distort, or shape public perception, regardless of the methods or accuracy of the information involved.

With a solid grasp of these key terms, we are now prepared to delve deeper into the mechanisms and historical context that have allowed misinformation to flourish. As we continue, we will explore how these concepts have evolved, how they influence public perception, and how they have shaped the social, political, and cultural dynamics of our time. By understanding the foundational elements of misinformation, we can better address the challenges it presents and work towards safeguarding the integrity of information in our societies.

Throughout this book, we will revisit these foundational concepts and reflect on the broader implications of all forms of information manipulation. We will examine how misinformation, disinformation, propaganda, and false narratives have all contributed to the complex challenges discussed throughout the book. This holistic perspective will help leave readers with an understanding that the book has addressed a wide spectrum of information issues, not just unintentional falsehoods, and underscore the importance of combating these challenges to preserve trust and integrity in our information ecosystems.

# 2

# The Rise of Information Manipulation

The spread of misinformation has become one of the defining challenges of the 21st century, significantly affecting societies across the globe. Digital platforms, particularly social media, have transformed the way people access information, but they have also created fertile ground for falsehoods to spread rapidly and broadly. This chapter aims to explore the emergence and evolution of misinformation—information that is false or misleading but not necessarily shared with harmful intent—and its wide-reaching implications on political, social, and cultural dynamics.

The year 2024 has been a stark reminder of how misinformation can take root and spread, often faster than accurate information can catch up. Imagine a hypothetical situation in which a notable incident occurs early in the year: a viral claim suggests that a major political candidate has made secretive deals with a foreign government, allegedly compromising national interests. Despite being debunked by credible sources, this misinformation spreads widely on social media, influencing public perception before the facts have a chance to gain traction.

This scenario exemplifies how misinformation continues to shape public opinion and ultimately impact political outcomes.

The proliferation of misinformation has far-reaching consequences. It can erode trust in institutions, polarize societies, and distort the public's understanding of important issues. In political contexts, misinformation is particularly damaging as it interferes with informed decision-making and weakens democratic processes. Beyond politics, misinformation also threatens public health, undermines scientific knowledge, and spreads confusion in educational contexts—all areas where accurate information is crucial for decision-making and maintaining societal trust.

This chapter will investigate the factors contributing to the rise of misinformation, such as the role of social media platforms, echo chambers, and algorithm-driven content distribution, which amplify false narratives and limit exposure to diverse perspectives. We will also define important concepts that are often conflated—like misinformation, disinformation (intentionally false information spread to deceive), and fake news—and explore how these have shaped the modern information landscape.

By examining the historical roots of misinformation, its psychological underpinnings, and the role of modern technology, we can better understand how false information spreads and impacts society. The chapter will also delve into efforts to counter misinformation, such as media literacy programs and fact-checking initiatives, and assess the challenges they face in an environment where misinformation spreads faster than ever before.

Ultimately, understanding the mechanisms that enable misinformation to flourish is crucial for developing effective responses. As individuals, institutions, and governments grapple with the complexities of misinformation, international collaboration, responsible technology development, and critical thinking skills emerge as essential tools in the effort to combat falsehoods and uphold truth in an increasingly interconnected world.

## 2.1 The Role of Social Media

Social media platforms have become key vehicles for the spread of misinformation, fundamentally altering the way false information circulates. These platforms—such as Facebook, X, TikTok, and YouTube—have revolutionized how people share and access information, making it easier for anyone to become both a consumer and producer of content. However, this democratization of information has also led to a surge in misinformation, with serious consequences for public perception, trust in institutions, and even public safety. This section explores how social media platforms have facilitated the spread of misinformation, the role of viral content, and the challenges involved in regulating false information.

### 2.1.1 The Spread of Misinformation on Social Media

One of the primary reasons social media has become a major conduit for misinformation is the **ease of sharing and the algorithmic design** of these platforms. Social media is designed to maximize user engagement, which often means prioritizing content that evokes strong emotional reactions—content that is more likely to be sensational, misleading, or outright false. Algorithms prioritize posts that generate likes, shares, and comments, leading to misinformation spreading far and wide at a rapid pace. The more engaging the content, the more likely it is to be promoted by the platform's algorithm, regardless of its accuracy.

For example, during the **COVID-19 pandemic**, false claims about unproven treatments or the supposed dangers of vaccines were widely shared across platforms like Facebook and X. These claims often contained emotionally charged language or imagery, making them more likely to be shared by users. As a result, misinformation about COVID-19 spread faster than the corrections provided by health authorities, undermining public trust in vaccines and contributing to vaccine hesitancy.

## 2.1.2 The Impact of Viral Content

The **virality** of content is a key factor in the spread of misinformation on social media. Viral content is designed to capture attention quickly, often through shocking headlines, sensational claims, or emotionally provocative messages. The problem with viral content is that its primary goal is to engage viewers, not to provide accurate information. As a result, misinformation often spreads far more effectively than factual content, which may be less sensational and therefore less likely to go viral.

Consider the example of the **2024 misinformation incident**, where a viral story claimed that a major political candidate had made clandestine deals with a foreign government. The emotionally charged nature of the claim led to widespread sharing before it could be debunked by credible news organizations. By the time the truth had caught up, the false narrative had already influenced public opinion. This incident demonstrates the power of viral content to shape perceptions, even when the information is later proven to be false.

### 2.1.3 Challenges of Regulating Misinformation

Regulating misinformation on social media is an immense challenge due to the **volume of content** and the **global nature** of these platforms. Social media companies have implemented various measures to combat misinformation, such as partnering with fact-checking organizations, flagging false information, and adjusting algorithms to reduce the spread of misleading content. However, these measures are often insufficient to fully address the problem.

**Automated content moderation** tools struggle to detect nuanced misinformation, such as satire or content that mixes true and false information. Human moderators, while more capable of understanding context, are overwhelmed by the sheer volume of posts that need to be reviewed. Moreover, misinformation can be culturally specific, meaning that a moderation approach that works in one region may not be effective in another. This is particularly problematic for global platforms like Facebook and TikTok, where misinformation can cross borders and impact diverse communities in different ways.

Another complication is the resistance to regulation from both users and social media companies. Users often perceive efforts to regulate misinformation as censorship, particularly when their posts are flagged or removed. This perception can lead to backlash against platforms and even increase the spread of misinformation, as users move to less-regulated alternative platforms that allow them to share content freely. Social media companies themselves have a financial incentive to keep users engaged, which may conflict with their efforts to limit the spread of sensational, yet false, content.

Shadowbanning is a practice employed by social media platforms where a user's content is deliberately restricted or hidden from wider visibility without their explicit knowledge. This often involves making posts less accessible or ensuring that they do not appear in search results or feeds. The intent is to limit the reach of accounts or posts that are flagged for violating platform guidelines, such as spreading misinformation or promoting harmful content. Shadowbanning is controversial because users may not be notified that their content is being suppressed, leading to concerns about transparency and fairness in how platforms enforce their rules.

**Demoting content** is another moderation strategy that involves reducing the visibility of certain posts. Instead of completely removing a post, platforms may use algorithms to ensure that it does not gain prominence in users' news feeds. Posts that are deemed potentially misleading or harmful may be pushed down, making them less likely to go viral. This method is seen as a middle-ground approach that avoids outright censorship while still curbing the spread of misinformation by limiting its reach.

**Content moderation** encompasses a broad range of activities aimed at managing the type of content that is allowed on a platform. It includes removing posts that explicitly violate policies, flagging content for fact-checking, and applying warning labels to posts that might contain misinformation. Moderation is conducted through a combination of automated algorithms and human review, each with its own limitations. Algorithms can act swiftly but may misidentify content, while human moderators bring nuanced judgment but can be overwhelmed by the volume of posts. The debate over content moderation often revolves around the tension between protecting free speech and the need to prevent harmful information from spreading, with critics pointing out biases or inconsistencies in enforcement, while advocates emphasize the importance of managing harmful or misleading narratives.

## 2.1.4 Real-World Examples

To understand the impact of social media on the spread of misinformation, it is crucial to consider specific examples. During the 2020 U.S. presidential election, misinformation regarding voter fraud proliferated on platforms such as X and Facebook. Despite numerous fact-checking efforts and corrections, many individuals continued to accept these false claims, which ultimately contributed to widespread distrust in the electoral process and played a role in the events of January 6th. This issue remains highly contentious, with strong partisan undertones—each side interpreting the situation differently from their respective viewpoints. This example underscores the challenges of containing misinformation once it becomes viral, especially when it aligns with users' pre-existing beliefs.

Another example is the spread of misinformation regarding **climate change**. False claims that climate change is a hoax or that scientific evidence supporting it is flawed have been widely shared on social media, often by individuals or groups with vested interests in opposing climate policies. These narratives have been amplified by social media algorithms and have contributed to public confusion about climate science, hindering efforts to address the climate crisis.

In the lead-up to the **2024 U.S. elections**, several instances of misinformation have been documented, illustrating the ongoing struggle to control false narratives on social media platforms. Here are a few examples:

- **Failed Moderation of Disinformation on Social Media**: Social media platforms such as Ticktock, Facebook, and YouTube have been tested for their ability to block election disinformation ads. Despite their efforts, Ticktock and Facebook approved several ads containing harmful and false information, such as misleading claims about voting procedures and calls for violence against electoral workers. The approval rates, despite some improvements since previous years, highlight the difficulty these platforms face in effectively moderating disinformation (Global Witness) Retrieved from: https://www.globalwitness.org/en/camp aigns/digital-threats/us-election-tiktok-and-facebook-fail-block-harmful-disinformation-youtube-succeeds/

- **Disinformation Dashboard Tracking**: The News Literacy Project has been actively tracking election misinformation through its "Misinformation Dashboard" to identify the tactics and topics of 2024 election misinformation. This tool aims to highlight the dangers misinformation poses to democracy and help people differentiate between factual news and misleading content (News Literacy Project) Retrieved from: https://misinfodashboard.newslit.org/

- **Continued Efforts by Foreign Actors**: Foreign interference in the 2024 U.S. elections remains a significant concern. Entities from countries such as Russia, China, and Iran have used social media to spread misleading information aimed at sowing discord and mistrust in the electoral process. These tactics often include disinformation campaigns and cyberattacks that exploit vulnerable voter populations.

These examples highlight the persistent and evolving challenge of controlling misinformation in the context of the 2024 elections. Despite increased awareness and improved content moderation policies, platforms still struggle to keep up with sophisticated tactics used by actors aiming to influence public perception and undermine election integrity.

## 2.1.5 The Role of Social Media Influencers

Another important aspect of how misinformation spreads on social media is the role of **influencers**. Social media influencers, who often have large followings, can significantly amplify misinformation, whether intentionally or unintentionally. Influencers may share misinformation because it aligns with their personal beliefs, because it generates engagement, or simply because they are unaware that the information is false.

Given their large audiences, the spread of misinformation by influencers can have a profound impact.

For instance, during the pandemic, several high-profile influencers shared misinformation about COVID-19 treatments, which was subsequently viewed by millions of followers. This misinformation not only spread rapidly but also gained credibility because it was endorsed by trusted figures, making it even harder for public health authorities to counter the false claims.

Social media platforms have become integral to the way people consume information, but their structure and incentives have also made them key vehicles for the spread of misinformation. The combination of algorithm-driven content, the virality of emotionally charged posts, challenges in regulating user-generated content, and the influence of prominent figures all contribute to the rapid dissemination of false information. Understanding the role of social media in the spread of misinformation is crucial for developing strategies to mitigate its impact and promote a more informed and resilient public.

Social media influencers have played a significant role in the **2024 U.S. elections**, with many politicians directly engaging with popular influencers and appearing on widely-followed podcasts to reach broader audiences. Here are some key examples:

- **Adoption of Influencer Strategies by Political Candidates**: In 2024, presidential candidates, like Donald Trump, and Kamala Harris, adopted influencer-like strategies to engage voters. They utilized platforms like TikTok and Instagram, often promoting campaign merchandise or sharing behind-the-scenes content to create a more relatable image. Donald Trump, for instance, used his social media accounts to create viral content, while Kamala Harris appeared on several popular podcasts to connect with younger voters, offering a direct and informal communication channel that traditional media could not provide. This tactic aimed to capture the attention of voters who primarily consume information online. Retrieved from https://news.northeastern.edu/2024/08/14/donald-trump-influencers/ Retrieved from: https://edition.cnn.com/2024/08/22/politics/content-creators- influencers-dnc-harris/index.html

· **The Role of Social Media Influencers in Political Engagement:** Platforms like TikTok, Reddit, Instagram, and Facebook became pivotal tools for political campaigns during the 2024 elections. Many influencers took active roles in political discussions, hosting live debates and interviews with political figures, including Kamala Harris, who appeared on TikTok videos and podcasts that catered to Gen Z audiences. This engagement helped shape political sentiment, as influencers became key voices in ongoing conversations across social media. Retrieved from https://www.pmg.com/insights/the-impact-of-social-media-on-the-2024-presidential-election

· **Influencers Changing Political Opinions**: According to a report by IZEA, 46% of social media users aged 18-60 reported changing their political opinions based on influencer content during the 2024 election. Furthermore, 82% of influencers planned to share their political views, and 87% used their platforms to promote voter registration and participation. Influencers became an essential channel for both Kamala Harris and Donald Trump, each appearing in influencer-led content to connect with different segments of the electorate. The growing role of influencer marketing in political engagement underscores its power to shape voter opinions. Retrieved from https://izea.com/press-releases/izea-insights-influencers-and-the-2024-election/

These examples demonstrate the increasingly influential role that social media influencers and platforms play in modern elections. Politicians, including Kamala Harris and Donald Trump, have utilized these platforms to reach younger audiences, amplify their campaign messages, and shape the political discourse in innovative ways.

## 2.2 Algorithms and Filter Bubbles

Social media algorithms play a crucial role in shaping the information landscape by determining what content users see in their feeds. These algorithms are designed to maximize engagement, often by showing users content that aligns with their existing beliefs and preferences. This process contributes to the creation of **filter bubbles**, where users are exposed primarily to information that reinforces their existing views while limiting exposure to diverse perspectives. This section will explore how algorithms and filter bubbles contribute to the spread of misinformation, particularly during the 2024 U.S. presidential election, and the challenges they pose to creating an informed electorate.

## 2.2.1 The Role of Algorithms in Information Curation

Algorithms on social media platforms like Facebook, X, and TikTok are programmed to keep users engaged by prioritizing content that is likely to resonate with them. This often means that users are shown content similar to what they have previously interacted with—whether through likes, shares, comments, or even time spent viewing certain posts. Leading up to the **2024 U.S. presidential election**, as well as in previous elections, this algorithmic curation played a significant role in reinforcing users' political beliefs, as supporters of each candidate were continuously fed content that aligned with their existing views.

For example, users who frequently engage with content supporting a particular candidate are more likely to see posts that reinforce that candidate's message, while opposing viewpoints are less likely to appear in their feeds. This **personalized content delivery** not only solidifies users' beliefs but also makes it difficult for them to access opposing perspectives, thereby deepening polarization. The algorithms' emphasis on engagement metrics inadvertently promotes sensationalist and often misleading content, as emotionally charged posts— whether true or false—tend to generate more interaction.

## 2.2.2 Filter Bubbles and Their Impact on Voter Perception

The concept of **filter bubbles** refers to the isolation of users within their own ideological echo chambers, created by the algorithmic curation of content. During the 2024 election year, filter bubbles have been particularly evident, as voters on both sides of the political spectrum have been exposed to vastly different narratives about key issues such as the economy, healthcare, and foreign policy. Supporters of each candidate have been presented with a version of reality that confirmed their biases, making it challenging for them to understand the broader political landscape or empathize with opposing viewpoints.

For instance, misinformation about **election integrity** has spread rapidly within filter bubbles. Supporters of one candidate have been repeatedly exposed to false claims that the election process was rigged, while supporters of the opposing candidate have seen content emphasizing the security and legitimacy of the election. These divergent narratives create parallel realities, with each group believing that their version of events is the absolute truth. The result is a fragmented electorate, where misinformation fuels distrust and division, making it difficult to achieve a shared understanding of the election outcome. Retrieved from: https://www.researchgate .net/publication/354459868_Filter_Bubbles_Echo_Chambe rs_and_Fake_News_How_Social_Media_Conditions_Indi viduals_to_Be_Less_Critical_of_Political_Misinformation

## 2.2.3 Real-World Data: The 2024 Election

Leading up to the 2024 presidential election, social media platforms have seen a significant uptick in the spread of politically charged misinformation, much of which was amplified by algorithms that prioritized engagement. According to a study by **Pew Research Center**, nearly **60% of voters** reported seeing misinformation about the election on social media platforms, and a large proportion of this misinformation was found to be circulating within specific filter bubbles. The study also found that users who primarily relied on social media for political news were more likely to hold inaccurate beliefs about the election compared to those who accessed news from a variety of sources.

In another survey **Pew Research Center** found that while most Americans are following the 2024 election closely, many find it challenging to determine what is true amidst the overwhelming coverage. About 73% report seeing inaccurate news about the election often, with Republicans more likely than Democrats to express difficulty in finding reliable information. The survey also highlights different levels of trust in news sources and fatigue over election coverage, showing deep partisan divides in how election news is consumed. Retrieved from https://www.pewresearch.org/journalism/2024/10/10/americans-views-of-2024-election-news/

Another report from **Media Matters** indicated that false claims about voter fraud and foreign interference were among the most widely shared posts in the weeks leading up to the election. These claims were particularly prevalent within politically homogeneous groups, where algorithms continued to feed users similar content, reinforcing their beliefs and making them more resistant to fact-checks and corrections. This cycle of reinforcement not only spread misinformation but also contributed to increased political polarization, as users became more entrenched in their views and less willing to engage with differing perspectives. Retrieved from: https://ww

w.mediamatters.org/google/youtube-has-allowed-conspirac
y-theories-about-interference-voting-machines-go-viral

## 2.2.4 The Challenge of Breaking Filter Bubbles

Breaking the influence of filter bubbles is a significant challenge, as it requires both changes in algorithmic design and shifts in user behavior. Social media platforms have experimented with measures to diversify the content users see, such as adjusting algorithms to include more content from outside users' immediate networks or highlighting posts from authoritative sources. However, these measures often face resistance from users who prefer content that aligns with their interests and beliefs.

Moreover, the business model of social media platforms, which relies on maximizing user engagement to generate advertising revenue, creates an inherent conflict of interest. Content that challenges users' beliefs is less likely to generate engagement, meaning that algorithms have little incentive to promote diverse perspectives. As a result, efforts to reduce the impact of filter bubbles and promote a more balanced information diet have had limited success.

Algorithms and filter bubbles are powerful forces in shaping the information landscape on social media. By curating content that aligns with users' existing beliefs, algorithms contribute to the creation of filter bubbles, where misinformation can thrive unchecked. During the 2024 U.S. presidential election, these dynamics played a significant role in spreading false information, deepening political divisions, and making it difficult for voters to access a balanced view of the issues. Addressing the challenges posed by algorithms and filter bubbles is essential for creating a more informed and less polarized public, but it requires concerted efforts from social media companies, policymakers, and users themselves.

## 2.3 Psychological Factors

**Psychological Factors** play a crucial role in explaining why individuals are susceptible to misinformation. Cognitive biases, emotional reactions, and social influences all contribute to the spread and acceptance of false information.

### 2.3.1 Confirmation Bias

**Confirmation bias** is the tendency for individuals to favor information that confirms their pre-existing beliefs or values while disregarding evidence that contradicts them. When people come across misinformation that aligns with their beliefs, they are more likely to accept and share it without critical evaluation.

- **Example**: In the 2020 and 2024 U.S. election cycles, individuals who already believed in widespread voter fraud were more likely to accept and share misinformation supporting these claims, regardless of the lack of evidence. Social media algorithms further amplified this bias by showing users content similar to what they had previously engaged with, creating echo chambers where misinformation thrived. Retrieved from https://www.researchgate.net/publicatio n/380730958_Election_Polls_on_Social_Media_Preval ence_Biases_and_Voter_Fraud_Beliefs

## 2.3.2 The Bandwagon Effect

The **bandwagon effect** refers to people's tendency to adopt certain behaviors or beliefs simply because others are doing so. On social media, when misinformation receives many likes, shares, or comments, it can create the illusion of credibility, prompting more users to believe it and pass it on.

- **Example**: During the COVID-19 pandemic, misinformation about unproven treatments like hydroxychloroquine gained traction because it was widely shared on platforms such as Facebook. The popularity of these posts created a bandwagon effect, leading more people to believe in and seek these treatments despite expert warnings. Retrieved from https://pmc.ncbi.nlm.nih.gov/articles/PMC9612566 /

## 2.3.3 Emotional Appeal

Misinformation often exploits emotions such as fear, anger, and empathy because these emotions can override people's ability to critically assess information. Emotional content is more likely to resonate deeply with individuals, prompting an instinctual reaction rather than a rational analysis. When individuals encounter emotionally provocative content, they are more inclined to share it without evaluating its accuracy, as the emotional impact creates a sense of urgency and immediacy.

For example, misinformation that evokes **fear**—such as rumors about health threats, dangers to children, or national security risks—taps into people's innate survival instincts. Fear-driven content can trigger a strong emotional response, leading people to spread the message quickly to warn others, regardless of whether it is factually correct. The 2020 COVID-19 pandemic demonstrated this dynamic clearly, as many people shared misinformation about unproven treatments or false claims about the origins of the virus out of fear for their safety and the well-being of their loved ones.

Similarly, misinformation that triggers **anger**—for instance, stories about political corruption or perceived injustices—can provoke outrage, causing individuals to share content to express their disapproval and rally support. This type of misinformation is particularly potent because anger is a mobilizing emotion that often compels people to take action, whether by spreading the information or joining a movement. During the 2024 U.S. election cycle, misinformation about alleged voter fraud spread widely, fueled by anger over perceived injustices and claims of compromised electoral integrity.

**Empathy**, on the other hand, can also be manipulated to spread misinformation. Content that portrays individuals or groups as victims in a compelling narrative can elicit empathy, prompting people to share the story out of a desire to support the victims or raise awareness. However, empathy-driven misinformation can be just as misleading as fear- or anger-based content. For example, emotionally charged misinformation about humanitarian crises, which may misrepresent the situation or assign blame inaccurately, can spread rapidly because people feel compelled to help.

Social media platforms further amplify the spread of emotionally charged misinformation due to their **engagement-focused algorithms**. These algorithms are designed to promote content that receives more interaction—likes, comments, and shares—which often means that emotionally engaging, sensational content is prioritized over more balanced, factual information. As a result, misinformation that exploits emotions spreads more widely, reinforcing individuals' beliefs and making it more challenging to counter with fact-based corrections.

In addition, **emotional contagion**—the tendency for people to "catch" emotions from others—plays a significant role in the viral spread of misinformation. When users see their friends or family members sharing emotionally charged content, they are more likely to react emotionally themselves and share the content further, contributing to a cascading effect that can rapidly spread misinformation across networks.

Understanding how emotions like fear, anger, and empathy drive the spread of misinformation is essential for developing strategies to combat it. Media literacy programs that teach people to recognize emotional manipulation and pause before sharing can be an effective tool in mitigating the spread of misinformation.

## 2.3.4. Cognitive Overload

The overwhelming amount of information available online can easily lead to **cognitive overload**, a state in which the sheer quantity of information exceeds an individual's capacity to process it effectively. In today's digital landscape, users are constantly bombarded with news articles, social media posts, videos, and advertisements. This constant influx of information can make it difficult for individuals to carefully evaluate the credibility of each piece of content they encounter. As a result, people may experience mental fatigue, reducing their ability to critically assess information and increasing the likelihood of relying on simplified decision-making processes.

When faced with cognitive overload, individuals often turn to **heuristic-based decision-making**, which involves using mental shortcuts to make quick judgments. Heuristics are efficient strategies that help people process information quickly but may lead to biased or incorrect conclusions. For example, an individual might decide that a post is trustworthy simply because it has been liked or shared by a large number of people, rather than evaluating the content for accuracy. This is known as the **popularity heuristic**, where people equate the popularity of a post with its credibility. Similarly, emotionally charged content can exploit another heuristic called the **affect heuristic**, where people use their emotional response to determine whether information is valid.

For instance, a **viral social media post** containing emotionally evocative images or language may be more likely to be believed and shared, regardless of its factual accuracy. The emotional impact of such content can bypass critical thinking, as individuals rely on their immediate feelings rather than a careful analysis of the content's credibility. During times of crisis, such as elections or public health emergencies, this heuristic-driven behavior can lead to the rapid spread of misinformation, as emotionally charged or sensational claims are more likely to attract attention and be shared widely.

**Social media algorithms** further exacerbate this problem by prioritizing content that generates high engagement, such as likes, shares, and comments. This means that emotionally engaging or popular content is more likely to be promoted, regardless of its factual accuracy. Consequently, individuals experiencing cognitive overload may be repeatedly exposed to the same misinformation, reinforcing their belief in its credibility through repeated exposure—a phenomenon known as the **illusory truth effect**. The more familiar a piece of information becomes, the more likely people are to perceive it as true, even if it is false.

Cognitive overload also affects individuals' ability to discern **credibility cues** such as the source of the information, the presence of evidence, or the expertise of the author. Instead of evaluating these factors, users may focus on superficial characteristics like the aesthetics of a website or the emotional tone of a headline. This makes it easier for misinformation to thrive, as misleading content can be designed to appear credible by mimicking legitimate news sources or using emotionally compelling narratives.

To mitigate the effects of cognitive overload, promoting **media literacy** is essential. Encouraging individuals to take a step back, verify the source of information, and be mindful of emotional manipulation can help reduce the reliance on heuristics and improve the quality of online information consumption. Additionally, technological solutions like fact-checking tools and browser extensions that provide credibility scores for websites can support users in making more informed decisions when confronted with an overwhelming amount of content.

## 2.3.5 False Consensus Effect

The **false consensus effect** is a cognitive bias in which individuals overestimate the extent to which their beliefs, values, or behaviors are shared by others. This bias leads people to believe that their views are more common or "normal" than they actually are, which can have significant implications for how misinformation spreads and is perceived.

When individuals encounter **misinformation** that aligns with their own views, the false consensus effect makes them more likely to assume that this information is widely accepted as true. This perceived consensus can create a **feedback loop**: because people believe that "everyone" thinks this way, they become more confident in their beliefs, and as a result, they are more inclined to share the information further. This cycle not only reinforces the misinformation among those who share it but also helps it spread to wider audiences, particularly in **homogeneous online communities** or **echo chambers**, where people predominantly engage with others who share similar views.

For example, during the **COVID-19 pandemic**, misinformation about vaccines, such as claims that they were harmful or part of a conspiracy, spread widely among certain online communities. Those who already distrusted vaccines or had doubts about their safety found this misinformation to be consistent with their existing beliefs. The false consensus effect led these individuals to assume that the majority of people shared their skepticism, which in turn reinforced their confidence in these false claims. Consequently, they were more likely to share this misinformation, contributing to the spread of vaccine hesitancy despite overwhelming scientific evidence supporting the safety and effectiveness of vaccines.

The false consensus effect is particularly **potent in social media environments**, where algorithms are designed to show users content similar to what they have previously engaged with. This **algorithmic reinforcement** creates a skewed perception of consensus, making individuals think that their beliefs are more widely held than they actually are. For instance, during elections, if users frequently engage with content promoting a particular political view, they are likely to see more of the same, leading them to believe that this viewpoint is the majority opinion. This perceived widespread acceptance can embolden individuals to share misinformation, believing they are simply echoing the views of the broader community.

Moreover, the false consensus effect can make people more resistant to **fact-checking** and corrections. If individuals believe that a majority of others agree with their perspective, they are likely to dismiss contrary information or evidence as being part of a biased minority view. This bias makes it challenging for corrective efforts to gain traction, as people may perceive fact-checks as an attempt to silence the majority rather than provide objective clarification.

The **social validation** aspect of the false consensus effect also plays a significant role in misinformation spread. When people believe that their views are widely shared, it provides them with a sense of belonging and validation, which further motivates them to continue sharing similar content. This sense of validation can be especially appealing when the information in question elicits strong emotions, such as fear or anger, which can override rational decision-making and make people more susceptible to spreading false information.

Understanding the false consensus effect is crucial for addressing the challenges of misinformation. Media literacy programs that encourage individuals to question their assumptions about consensus and recognize the diversity of perspectives can help counteract this bias. Additionally, algorithmic transparency and diversity in content exposure can help reduce the impact of false consensus by providing users with a broader range of viewpoints, thus challenging the perception that their views are universally held.

Psychological factors such as confirmation bias, the bandwagon effect, emotional appeal, cognitive overload, and the false consensus effect all contribute to the susceptibility to misinformation. Social media platforms, with their engagement-focused algorithms, further amplify these biases, making it difficult for individuals to discern credible information from false narratives. Understanding these psychological mechanisms is crucial in developing effective strategies to counter misinformation and promote media literacy.

## 2.4 Misinformation in Political Campaigns

**Misinformation in Political Campaigns** has become a significant factor that influences elections and undermines public trust in democratic processes. Misinformation—false or misleading information shared without a clear intent to deceive—has been used in political campaigns to sway public opinion, confuse voters, and create division. It can take many forms, from spreading false claims about candidates or policies to manipulating public perception through misleading or incomplete information. This misinformation often works in tandem with **election interference**, where both domestic and foreign actors seek to influence electoral outcomes through underhanded tactics.

### 2.4.1 Impact of Misinformation on Political Campaigns and Elections

Misinformation in political campaigns is often designed to provoke strong emotional reactions, such as fear, anger, or distrust. These emotional responses can override critical thinking, leading voters to believe and act upon misleading information without verifying its accuracy. This is particularly dangerous in the context of **political campaigns**, as misinformation can distort public perception of candidates and their policies, ultimately influencing voter behavior.

For example, during the **2016 and 2020 U.S. presidential elections**, misinformation about voter fraud, hacked voting machines, and baseless claims about certain candidates' affiliations spread widely on social media platforms like X and Facebook. The misinformation often targeted specific groups, such as undecided voters or minorities, with the intent to dissuade them from voting or to push them towards a particular candidate. By creating confusion about voting procedures or making exaggerated claims about voter suppression, misinformation can undermine voter confidence and contribute to lower voter turnout.

In the **2024 U.S. elections**, similar patterns of misinformation have emerged, further complicating the political landscape. Social media platforms have struggled to moderate and remove false information, which often spreads faster than accurate news due to its sensational nature. The misinformation leading up to the 2024 election has largely focused on claims of voter fraud, foreign interference, and personal attacks on candidates. These narratives, once entrenched, are challenging to dispel, and efforts by fact-checkers are often met with skepticism, particularly when misinformation aligns with users' pre-existing beliefs.

The rise of **deepfake technology** has also had a profound effect on misinformation in political campaigns. Deepfakes—videos altered using artificial intelligence to make someone appear to say or do something they didn't—have been used to mislead voters. In some instances, deepfake videos purportedly showed political candidates making controversial statements, which then went viral on social media before being debunked. The damage caused by such misinformation is often difficult to reverse, as many voters retain negative impressions despite corrections.

## 2.4.2 Election Interference

Election interference, which can include the use of misinformation, takes various forms, each with the goal of undermining electoral integrity, influencing outcomes, or damaging public trust in democratic institutions. These forms include:

- **Disinformation Campaigns**: Disinformation is intentionally false information spread to deceive and manipulate public perception. Foreign actors, such as **Russia, China, and Iran**, have been implicated in disinformation campaigns aimed at influencing elections in Western democracies. For example, in the 2016 U.S. election, Russian operatives used social media platforms to spread disinformation supporting specific candidates while attacking others, thereby polarizing the electorate and eroding trust in democratic processes.
- **Hacking and Cyberattacks**: Cyberattacks are a direct form of election interference, where hackers target electoral infrastructure, such as voter registration databases, to disrupt the voting process or steal sensitive information. In the lead-up to the 2024 elections, U.S. officials have reported several attempted cyberattacks on state election systems by foreign actors, though most attempts were successfully repelled. These attacks are aimed at creating distrust in the election's security, causing voters to question the legitimacy of the outcomes.
- **Social Media Influence Operations**: Influence operations involve the use of social media to sway public sentiment, often using fake accounts or bots to amplify messages. During

the 2020 election cycle, multiple accounts linked to foreign governments were found to be sharing misinformation related to election fraud and the integrity of the voting process. These influence campaigns are designed to create confusion and deepen political divisions, making it difficult for voters to discern fact from fiction.

- **Astroturfing**: Astroturfing is a tactic where a group or organization creates the appearance of grassroots support for a cause. During elections, astroturfing can involve creating fake groups that appear to be comprised of regular citizens but are actually funded and managed by political organizations or foreign actors. These fake groups spread misinformation to sway public opinion and influence voting behavior.
- **Deepfake Propaganda**: The use of deepfakes to spread mis-information about political candidates is another form of election interference. These highly realistic, AI-generated videos can mislead voters by portraying candidates as saying or doing things they have not. Deepfakes can easily go viral, especially when they trigger strong emotional responses, making them an effective tool for manipulating public perception and sowing confusion during election periods.

## 2.4.3 Public Trust and Democratic Processes

The combined effect of misinformation and election interfer-ence has significantly undermined public trust in democratic institutions. When voters struggle to differentiate between credible information and falsehoods, their faith in the electoral process weakens, leading to skepticism and apathy. This issue has become increasingly evident in recent elections, including in the 2024 U.S. election cycle, where widespread misinformation campaigns about voter fraud, rigged voting machines, and foreign interference have resurfaced and created an atmosphere of distrust. As a result, many voters have begun to question the legitimacy of future election results, regardless of evidence supporting the integrity of the process.

This decline in trust has several far-reaching consequences. First, it **deepens political polarization** by amplifying divisive narratives. People become more entrenched in their views, which are often based on misinformation that supports their biases. For instance, misinformation about the 2016, 2020 and 2024 election cycles has led to further fragmentation within the electorate, with different groups believing entirely different versions of events, often supported by unverified claims circulating on social media. This kind of polarization creates a toxic political environment where constructive dialogue becomes nearly impossible.

**Lower voter turnout** is another consequence of declining trust in democratic institutions. When people believe that elections are rigged or that their votes will not be counted accurately, they are less likely to participate in the electoral process. This disengagement erodes the foundation of democracy, which relies on widespread citizen participation to ensure that elected representatives genuinely reflect the will of the people. In the **2024 US presidential race**, reports have indicated a noticeable decline in voter enthusiasm among certain demographics, attributed in part to widespread misinformation that undermined confidence in the electoral process. Retrieved from: https://to day.yougov.com/politics/articles/49987-disengaged-voters-role-2024-election-biden-trump-poll

The erosion of trust can also lead to **civil unrest**, as seen in the **George Floyd protests in 2020**. While primarily sparked by issues of racial injustice and police brutality, the unrest was also fueled by a deep-seated mistrust of law enforcement and government accountability, further exacerbated by misinformation and inflammatory narratives on social media. Many false claims circulated about the events surrounding George Floyd's death and subsequent protests, which escalated tensions and contributed to the widespread demonstrations, at time violent, across the United States.

Misinformation and election interference have become **powerful tools for those seeking to exploit vulnerabilities in democratic systems**. These tactics can be used by both foreign and domestic actors to destabilize democracies, weaken political opponents, and promote authoritarian agendas. Foreign actors, like Russia, China, and Iran, have been implicated in efforts to influence Western elections through misinformation and cyberattacks, aiming to sow division and undermine democratic values. These efforts often target specific voter groups with tailored misinformation, further polarizing society and weakening trust in the democratic process.

## 2.4.4 Election Interference

Election interference is not limited to the spread of misinformation. There are multiple forms that collectively threaten the integrity of democratic processes:

- **Disinformation Campaigns**: These involve the intentional spread of false information to manipulate voters' beliefs about a candidate, the voting process, or key election issues. Social media and online forums are common avenues for disinformation campaigns, but traditional media can also play a role.  For example, false narratives about election fraud were widely spread during the 2020 and 2024 U.S. elections, fueling public distrust and polarizing the electorate.
- **Cyberattacks**: Hackers may target electoral infrastructure, such as voter registration databases or voting systems, to cause disruption or manipulate voting results. In addition, cyberattacks can be used to access and leak campaign emails, often selectively, to paint a particular candidate or party in a negative light. Such was the case during the 2016 U.S. presidential election when campaign emails were hacked and released, influencing public perception of the candidates.
- **Financial Influence**:  Foreign or domestic actors can use financial resources to influence elections by funding particular campaigns or political action committees (PACs). This financial support may be given covertly, skirting campaign finance laws to exert influence over the election outcome. Such interference can lead to an imbalance in campaign resources, where some candidates gain unfair advantages through illicit funding.
- **Voter Suppression Tactics**: Voter suppression can also be a form of election interference, where misinformation about voting times, locations, or eligibility is used to deter certain

groups from voting. Cyberattacks may also be employed to manipulate voter rolls or disrupt the voting process, reducing voter turnout in targeted demographics. During the 2024 elections, misinformation about mail-in voting and polling hours led to confusion, particularly among minority and rural voters, suppressing their participation.

- **Fake Grassroots Movements (Astroturfing)**: These involve the creation of artificial movements that appear to be grassroots campaigns but are, in fact, orchestrated by political groups or foreign actors. These fake movements can be used to create an illusion of widespread support for a particular issue or candidate, thus misleading the public about the level of genuine political support. Astroturfing is often supported by disinformation campaigns and is intended to manipulate the political narrative.

## 2.4.4.1 Consequences of Election Interference

The consequences of misinformation and election interference are profound, with several damaging effects on democracy:

- **Undermining Trust**: One of the most significant consequences is the erosion of public trust in the electoral process. When voters believe that elections are manipulated—whether by foreign interference, disinformation, or other tactics—it diminishes their confidence in the fairness of democracy and in the legitimacy of elected leaders. This decline in trust has been evident in the increasing skepticism about election outcomes in recent years.

- **Polarization**: Disinformation campaigns often exploit and deepen existing societal divisions, leading to greater political polarization. This further erodes the potential for civil discourse and cooperation between different political groups, creating a toxic environment where common ground becomes increasingly hard to find. The polarization caused by misinformation contributes to social instability and makes democratic governance more challenging.
- **Threat to Sovereignty**: Election interference by foreign actors represents a direct threat to a nation's sovereignty. When foreign entities manipulate electoral outcomes, they undermine the autonomy of a country's political system, infringing on the ability of its citizens to freely choose their leaders without external influence.

## 2.4.4.2 Combating Election Interference

To protect democratic integrity, several strategies are being employed to combat election interference:

- **Enhanced Cybersecurity**: Securing election infrastructure—such as voter databases, voting machines, and campaign systems—is crucial for preventing cyberattacks. Governments and election authorities are investing in robust cybersecurity measures and collaborating with technology companies to identify and mitigate potential threats. The Cybersecurity and Infrastructure Security Agency (CISA) in the United States has been at the forefront of safeguarding electoral infrastructure against cyber threats.

- **Media Literacy Programs**: Educating the public on how to identify disinformation and misinformation can significantly reduce their effectiveness. Media literacy programs aim to teach voters how to critically evaluate information, verify sources, and recognize common tactics used in disinformation campaigns. These programs are vital in empowering citizens to become more discerning consumers of information.

- **International Cooperation**: Election interference is a global issue, requiring cooperation among countries to effectively combat it. International partnerships, such as the sharing of intelligence on cyber threats, are essential to counteract interference efforts by foreign actors. The European Union, for example, has established initiatives to counter foreign influence, including creating task forces dedicated to identifying and countering disinformation.

## 2.5 Conclusion

Election interference, through tactics such as disinformation campaigns, cyberattacks, financial manipulation, voter suppression, and astroturfing, poses a severe threat to the integrity of democratic processes worldwide. These actions not only undermine public trust in electoral outcomes but also weaken the foundations of democracy itself. As technology evolves, so do the tactics used by those who seek to influence elections, making constant vigilance, international collaboration, and proactive measures essential in safeguarding democracy. Addressing these challenges requires a multifaceted approach that involves securing electoral infrastructure, promoting media literacy, and fostering international cooperation to ensure that elections remain free, fair, and representative of the will of the people.

# 3

# Historical Context of Information Manipulation

Throughout history, **manipulating information** has been used as a powerful tool to manipulate, oppress, suppress and control populations, influence opinions, and gain political or social advantage. **Suppression** means preventing something from happening or being expressed, such as restricting speech, ideas, or protests. For example, suppressing a protest could involve prohibiting public gatherings or removing related social media posts. **Oppression** refers to prolonged and systemic control or mistreatment of individuals or groups, often through unjust authority. It involves denying rights and opportunities, such as racial or gender oppression, which keeps certain groups marginalized through systemic discrimination and coercion.

It is for this very reason that it is vital to recognize that misinformation—the spread of false or misleading information without necessarily having the intent to deceive—has been present in nearly every society, long before the advent of digital technology. From ancient rulers and medieval religious leaders to 19th-century newspaper magnates and 20th-century governments, misinformation has served as a means to shape narratives, consolidate power, and control the flow of information.

In the ancient and medieval eras, misinformation often took the form of **rumors and myths** spread by rulers to justify their authority or vilify their opponents. For instance, political leaders in ancient Rome and Greece frequently employed misinformation to bolster their public image or discredit their rivals. During the Middle Ages, **religious misinformation** played a key role, with narratives crafted to maintain the authority of the church and suppress dissenting views. These early examples illustrate that misinformation has always been a fundamental element of human society, used by those in power to protect their interests.

The invention of the **printing press** in the 15th century marked a pivotal moment in the history of misinformation, as it allowed false narratives to be distributed to a much wider audience than ever before. The **Reformation** and **Counter-Reformation** are notable examples of how misinformation and propaganda were used to sway public opinion and control the narrative during religious conflicts. Pamphlets containing misleading or sensational information were used by both sides to promote their viewpoints and undermine the credibility of their opponents.

The **19th century** saw the rise of **mass media** and the birth of **yellow journalism**—a type of journalism that relies on sensationalism and exaggeration to attract readers. During this period, newspaper publishers, such as William Randolph Hearst, used misinformation to shape public opinion on political issues and even incite conflicts, such as the **Spanish-American War**. This marked a significant evolution in how misinformation was used, transitioning from more localized, rumor-based tactics to large-scale, media-driven campaigns that reached millions of people.

In the **20th century**, misinformation became an integral part of **state propaganda** during both World Wars and the **Cold War**. Governments utilized misinformation to rally public support, demonize enemies, and maintain control over domestic populations. The Nazi regime in Germany, under the direction of **Joseph Goebbels**, used misinformation and propaganda extensively to justify their actions, vilify minority groups, and control the German population. Similarly, during the Cold War, both the United States and the Soviet Union used misinformation to gain a strategic advantage and win the battle for public perception.

With the advent of the **digital age** in the late 20th and early 21st centuries, the nature of misinformation evolved yet again, becoming more sophisticated and far-reaching due to the rise of the internet and social media platforms. The ability for misinformation to spread rapidly and reach a global audience has made it more challenging than ever to combat. The **early 2000s** saw the rise of email chains and online forums, which allowed misinformation to spread easily across different segments of society. This laid the groundwork for the more advanced forms of online misinformation that we see today, such as **deepfakes**, conspiracy theories, and **fake news** shared on social media platforms.

In this chapter, we explore the historical context of misinformation by examining several key periods. These include ancient and medieval times, the printing press and Reformation era, the age of mass media and yellow journalism, the propaganda campaigns of the World Wars, the information warfare of the

Cold War. The evolution of misinformation in the digital age. By understanding the historical use of misinformation, we can better appreciate its enduring role in shaping societies and recognize the challenges it presents in the modern era.

This historical journey will help us understand that misinformation is not a new problem—it has simply adapted to each new communication technology, growing in sophistication and reach. Understanding these historical patterns is crucial for addressing the current challenges posed by misinformation in our hyper-connected world.

## 3.1 Information Manipulation in Ancient and Medieval Times

In ancient times, political leaders and rulers often relied on **misinformation** to consolidate power, manipulate public perception, and maintain control over their populations. This form of manipulation involved spreading **false narratives** that portrayed rulers as divinely appointed or having supernatural powers, thereby legitimizing their authority and reinforcing their right to rule. By crafting these narratives, leaders could secure the loyalty and obedience of their people, often stifling dissent and uniting the population under a single, powerful image.

For instance, in **Ancient Egypt**, pharaohs were portrayed as gods or representatives of gods on Earth, which was a strategic way of controlling the people. By creating an aura of divine power, they ensured that the populace viewed them as untouchable and beyond reproach, discouraging rebellion and dissent. This manipulation of public belief through religious and political propaganda allowed rulers to maintain their power for generations.

Similarly, in the **Roman Empire**, emperors like **Augustus** carefully crafted their public image using a combination of propaganda and misinformation. Augustus portrayed himself as the "restorer of the Republic" while, in reality, consolidating power to become Rome's first emperor. He used poets like **Virgil** to propagate myths that connected his rule to the destiny of Rome, weaving a narrative that served to validate his authority. By controlling the flow of information, Augustus managed to secure popular support and avoid the perception that he was undermining Rome's republican traditions.

Ancient rulers also used misinformation to weaken their enemies. Alexander the Great was known to spread false information to confuse rival armies and create divisions among opposing factions. This tactic allowed him to face opponents that were already destabilized by rumors and misinformation, giving him a strategic advantage on the battlefield.

In the **medieval period**, misinformation played a significant role in religious contexts, particularly in maintaining **religious authority** and controlling public behavior. Religious leaders often used misinformation to ensure the church's power remained unchallenged, guiding public opinion on religious doctrines and practices. This practice involved spreading carefully curated narratives, suppressing dissenting views, and labeling alternative interpretations of doctrine as **heresy**.

For example, during the **Middle Ages**, the Catholic Church disseminated misinformation to bolster its authority and control over Europe. Religious leaders used **fear of heresy** as a tool to suppress any beliefs that deviated from official church teachings. By branding alternative viewpoints as heretical, the church was able to delegitimize dissenters, often leading to their excommunication, imprisonment, or even execution. The **Inquisition** was a notorious manifestation of this practice, where misinformation about the supposed dangers of heretical beliefs was used to justify the persecution and punishment of those who opposed church doctrine.

The spread of **relics** and **indulgences** also involved a degree of misinformation. The church often promoted the idea that possessing certain relics or purchasing indulgences could bring spiritual benefits or reduce time in **purgatory**. These claims, which were often exaggerated or unfounded, were used to extract wealth from the population and reinforce the church's influence over their spiritual lives. People were led to believe in the tangible benefits of these practices, which maintained their loyalty to the church and generated significant financial gain.

Religious misinformation also played a role in **crusades**. The call for the **First Crusade** in 1095 by Pope **Urban II** included misinformation about the treatment of Christian pilgrims in the Holy Land, as well as exaggerations of the atrocities committed by Muslims. This was used to generate support for the crusade and mobilize Christian armies under the banner of religious duty. The misinformation fueled hatred and a sense of urgency among European Christians, driving thousands to join the effort to reclaim the Holy Land.

# 3.2 The Printing Press and the Spread of Propaganda

The invention of the **printing press** by **Johannes Gutenberg** in the mid-15th century marked a major turning point in the spread of information, including misinformation. Before the printing press, the dissemination of ideas was limited to hand-copied manuscripts, which were labor-intensive and accessible only to a small portion of society. With the printing press, it became possible to produce books, pamphlets, and other printed material on a mass scale, dramatically increasing the availability of information. This newfound ability to spread written content quickly and broadly transformed how ideas, both truthful and misleading, reached the public.

One significant impact of the printing press was its role in spreading **false narratives** and **propaganda**. The technology allowed for the rapid dissemination of information without a system for verifying the accuracy of the content, which made it much easier for **misinformation** and **disinformation** to spread. Political leaders, religious authorities, and other influential figures used the printing press to distribute materials that supported their agendas, regardless of the truthfulness of the content. This ability to quickly distribute printed propaganda meant that misinformation could now shape public opinion on a much larger scale, ultimately influencing politics, religion, and culture.

For example, political pamphlets often contained **exaggerations** or outright **falsehoods** about opponents. The availability of the printing press made it possible for rival factions to launch misinformation campaigns aimed at discrediting each other.

This phenomenon helped lay the groundwork for the use of mass media as a tool for propaganda, influencing large groups of people through targeted messages.

The **Protestant Reformation** and the **Catholic Counter-Reformation** are key historical examples of how the printing press was used to spread **propaganda** and misinformation to sway public opinion. The Reformation, initiated by **Martin Luther** in 1517, was significantly fueled by the ability of the printing press to spread ideas rapidly across Europe. Luther's **95 Theses**, which criticized various practices of the Catholic Church, were printed and distributed widely, reaching a far larger audience than would have been possible through traditional means.

The Reformation saw a proliferation of pamphlets, woodcuts, and translations of the Bible, which were used to spread messages critical of the Catholic Church. Many of these materials contained **misinformation** designed to undermine the authority of the church and persuade the general population to support the Reformation. For example, **anti-Catholic pamphlets** often depicted church leaders as corrupt and immoral, exaggerating or fabricating stories of excess and abuse. These materials played a crucial role in shaping public perception and mobilizing support for the Reformation movement.

In response, the **Catholic Counter-Reformation** also relied heavily on the printing press to combat the spread of Protestant ideas. The Catholic Church produced **propaganda** intended to defend its practices and discredit Protestant leaders. The **Index Librorum Prohibitorum** (List of Prohibited Books) was established to control the flow of information and suppress heretical writings. The church also commissioned **pro-Catholic pamphlets** and works that aimed to counter the arguments made by Protestant reformers. These materials often contained **misleading narratives** that portrayed Protestant leaders as heretics leading people astray, and they sought to reinforce the legitimacy and moral authority of the Catholic Church.

During this period, the use of **visual propaganda** was also notable. Woodcuts and engravings were powerful tools that could communicate messages effectively to an audience that might not be literate. The Protestant and Catholic factions both used these visual media to evoke emotional responses, often depicting opponents in **grotesque or threatening ways**. This visual misinformation played a key role in shaping public sentiment and deepening divisions between Catholics and Protestants.

The **printing press** not only amplified the spread of genuine religious debate but also became a critical tool for spreading **false or exaggerated claims** that fueled religious conflict. This era of **religious turmoil** demonstrated how access to mass-produced information could empower movements but also escalate conflicts, as propaganda and misinformation spread unchecked across Europe. The ease of printing made it difficult for any centralized authority to control the narrative completely, leading to an information landscape that was dynamic, contested, and often unreliable.


## 3.3 Misinformation in the Age of Revolutions


The **American** and **French Revolutions** were pivotal events in the late 18th century, fueled in large part by the strategic use of **pamphlets, propaganda, and rumors**. These forms of communication were instrumental in rallying support, spreading revolutionary ideas, and inciting public anger against the ruling authorities.

In the **American Revolution**, pamphlets played a crucial role in mobilizing colonists against British rule. One of the most famous pamphlets, **Thomas Paine's "Common Sense"** (1776), effectively used persuasive language to argue for independence from Britain. Paine's pamphlet contained both facts and emotional appeals, designed to galvanize colonial sentiment against the British monarchy. Although "Common Sense" was largely truthful, it also exaggerated British injustices and portrayed independence as the only reasonable course of action, simplifying a complex political situation into a stark battle between freedom and tyranny. Such pamphlets often relied on **emotional rhetoric** to stir revolutionary fervor, thereby influencing public opinion and prompting collective action.

Additionally, **rumors and misinformation** were widespread during the American Revolution. British actions, such as the **Boston Massacre**, were reported in ways that incited outrage among colonists. While some reports were accurate, others exaggerated the brutality of the British forces, portraying them as villains who indiscriminately harmed innocent colonists. These narratives helped build a unified anti-British sentiment among diverse colonial populations, making them more likely to support the revolutionary cause.

The **French Revolution** similarly relied on pamphlets and rumors to create revolutionary momentum. **Revolutionary leaders** used pamphlets to criticize the French monarchy, depict King Louis XVI and Queen Marie Antoinette as corrupt and out of touch with the people, and spread ideas about equality and liberty. The **"Affair of the Diamond Necklace"** scandal, for example, was used to paint Marie Antoinette as greedy and indifferent to the suffering of the French people, even though much of the story was fabricated or exaggerated. This misinformation was instrumental in eroding the monarchy's legitimacy and turning the public against the royal family.

The role of **propaganda and rumors** in the French Revolution cannot be overstated. **Revolutionary leaders**, including the **Jacobins**, used sensational pamphlets and posters to incite anger against the aristocracy and encourage support for radical reforms. The spread of rumors about secret plots by the nobility and foreign interventions fueled a climate of fear and distrust, which ultimately led to events like the **Reign of Terror**, during which many perceived enemies of the revolution were executed based on exaggerated or false accusations.

After the turmoil of the French Revolution, **Napoleon Bonaparte** rose to power, largely by capitalizing on his military successes and through an effective propaganda machine that manipulated public perception. Napoleon understood the power of **controlling information** and used **misinformation and censorship** to maintain his authority and shape public opinion in his favor.

One of the key strategies Napoleon employed was to **control the press**. He established a strict **censorship regime**, shutting down newspapers that were critical of his rule and ensuring that only favorable accounts of his actions were published. By reducing the number of independent newspapers and consolidating control over the press, Napoleon was able to tightly manage the flow of information. He also created his own state-sponsored publications, which praised his achievements and presented him as a heroic figure who was leading France to greatness.

Napoleon was also known for using **misleading narratives**

to portray his military campaigns as victories, even when they were strategic withdrawals or stalemates. He carefully crafted **bulletins** from the battlefield, which were published in French newspapers, exaggerating his successes and downplaying any setbacks. This form of misinformation helped maintain public morale and support for his regime, even during difficult times. For example, after the **disastrous Russian campaign** of 1812, Napoleon's reports to the French public minimized the extent of the losses and framed the retreat as a strategic regrouping, rather than a catastrophic defeat.

Napoleon also employed **visual propaganda** to build his image. He commissioned artists to create paintings and statues that depicted him in an idealized light, often portraying him as a defender of the revolution and the embodiment of French strength. These images were disseminated throughout France to create a **cult of personality** around him, ensuring that the public viewed him as the rightful leader of the nation. This visual propaganda helped to cultivate loyalty among the population, despite the significant hardships they endured due to Napoleon's military ambitions.

Additionally, **Napoleon's censorship** extended to books and plays that criticized his policies or portrayed him in a negative light. He controlled the narrative around his rise to power and his role as Emperor of France, ensuring that dissenting voices were silenced. By shaping how history was recorded and how current events were reported, Napoleon effectively used misinformation to craft a version of reality that suited his political ambitions.

## 3.4 The Rise of Mass Media and Yellow Journalism

The **late 19th century** saw a significant transformation in the media landscape, particularly in the United States, with the emergence of **yellow journalism**. Yellow journalism is a term used to describe a style of newspaper reporting that emphasized **sensationalism** over factual accuracy, often using exaggerated or misleading headlines and content to attract readers. The goal of yellow journalism was not necessarily to inform the public with objective news but rather to capture attention and increase newspaper sales, often by stirring emotions like fear, anger, or excitement.

Yellow journalism emerged as **newspaper publishers** competed fiercely for readership. This competition was most famously illustrated by the rivalry between **Joseph Pulitzer's New York World** and **William Randolph Hearst's New York Journal**. Both publishers were known for their use of sensational headlines, dramatic illustrations, and emotionally charged stories that often bent or completely disregarded the truth. The term "yellow journalism" itself was coined in reference to a popular comic strip character, the "Yellow Kid," who appeared in Pulitzer's and later Hearst's papers, symbolizing the sensational and attention-grabbing nature of this type of journalism.

The content of yellow journalism often focused on **scandal, crime, and melodrama**, with stories crafted to elicit strong emotional reactions. Reports were frequently embellished or distorted to create excitement and outrage, and these stories contributed to shaping public opinion by offering readers a skewed version of reality. The sensationalized approach to news had a significant impact on public perception, as many readers took these stories at face value, unaware of the exaggeration or outright misinformation involved.

Yellow journalism also played a role in popularizing **penny press newspapers**, which were inexpensive and therefore accessible to a broader audience, including the working class. This accessibility allowed yellow journalism to reach a wide readership, influencing public opinion on a range of issues, including politics, social issues, and international affairs. As a result, yellow journalism had a profound impact on the formation of public attitudes and beliefs, contributing to the shaping of the collective consciousness of the time.

**Case Study: The Role of Yellow Journalism in Inciting the Spanish-American War:** One of the most famous examples of yellow journalism's influence on public opinion and international events is its role in **inciting the Spanish-American War** in 1898. In the late 1800s, the United States had growing economic and political interests in Cuba, which was then a Spanish colony. The Cuban struggle for independence from Spain became a major news story, and yellow journalists were quick to capitalize on the dramatic elements of the conflict.

**William Randolph Hearst** and **Joseph Pulitzer** used their newspapers to publish exaggerated and often false accounts of Spanish atrocities against the Cuban people. These stories were designed to generate outrage among the American public, portraying the Spanish as brutal oppressors and the Cubans as helpless victims in need of American intervention. The headlines were often highly inflammatory, such as "Cuban Babes in Blood" or "Spanish Cannibalism," aimed at inciting emotional responses and rallying public support for the Cuban cause.

A critical moment in the lead-up to the Spanish-American War was the **explosion of the USS Maine** in Havana Harbor in February 1898. The incident resulted in the deaths of 266 American sailors, and while the cause of the explosion was unclear, Hearst and Pulitzer seized the opportunity to publish sensational stories blaming Spain for the attack, despite a lack of evidence. Hearst famously used the headline, "**Remember the Maine, to Hell with Spain!**" to inflame public sentiment and call for war. The newspapers' relentless coverage, filled with sensational claims and patriotic rhetoric, created immense pressure on the U.S. government to take action.

The influence of yellow journalism on the Spanish-American War demonstrates how the power of sensationalized reporting can lead to significant real-world consequences. The inflammatory stories and headlines published by Hearst and Pulitzer helped sway American public opinion toward supporting military intervention in Cuba, eventually leading to a declaration of war against Spain in April 1898. President **William McKinley**, who had initially been reluctant to enter the conflict, faced mounting public pressure as a result of the widespread outrage fueled by yellow journalism. The war, which lasted only a few months, resulted in a decisive victory for the United States and marked the beginning of American imperial expansion.

The **Spanish-American War** is a clear example of how **yellow journalism** leveraged misinformation and exaggerated narratives to influence public perception and push for political action. The use of sensationalism not only sold newspapers but also shaped foreign policy, ultimately leading to a conflict that reshaped the geopolitical landscape of the Americas. It highlights the impact that media can have in stoking nationalism and guiding public sentiment toward specific outcomes, often at the expense of factual reporting.

## 3.5 Propaganda During the World Wars

**World War I** was one of the first major conflicts in which **propaganda** and **misinformation** were used on a massive scale by all parties involved. Governments recognized that controlling information was crucial to maintaining morale, rallying public support, and demonizing the enemy. Propaganda efforts involved not only promoting the war effort but also creating a narrative that justified the conflict and vilified the opposition.

- **Demonizing the Enemy**: During World War I, **demonization of the enemy** was a key propaganda tactic. For example, British and French propaganda depicted German soldiers as barbaric and inhumane, often using emotionally charged imagery to portray them as "Huns" committing atrocities. **Posters and pamphlets** circulated stories—some based on facts, others fabricated—about German soldiers committing brutal acts, such as the killing of civilians, the mistreatment of prisoners, and the destruction of towns. One infamous example was the **"Rape of Belgium"** narrative, which exaggerated German actions in Belgium to stoke anger and hatred among the Allied populations. This type of misinformation served to unite the public against a common enemy by portraying the Germans as a threat to civilization itself.
- **Boosting Morale and Recruitment**: Propaganda during

World War I was also used to **boost morale** on the home front and encourage enlistment. Governments issued posters that glorified military service, often depicting soldiers as heroic and noble defenders of freedom and national honor. British propaganda, for example, used the famous **"Your Country Needs You"** poster featuring Lord Kitchener to motivate young men to enlist. The American government followed suit with posters like **"Uncle Sam Wants You"**, appealing to citizens' patriotism and sense of duty. These campaigns often omitted the harsh realities of war, instead focusing on idealized images of courage and valor to sustain public support.

- **Controlling Information**: Governments also employed **censorship** to suppress any information that could damage morale or question the legitimacy of the war. Newspapers were heavily monitored, and journalists were often prevented from reporting negative aspects of the war, such as high casualties or poor conditions on the front lines. Instead, the media focused on victories, downplayed losses, and presented an overly optimistic view of the progress of the war. This control over information allowed governments to maintain a positive narrative and prevent dissent from spreading among the population.
- **Misinformation Campaigns**: During World War I, misinformation campaigns were also used to confuse and mislead the enemy. The use of **false reports** about troop movements and battlefield plans was a common tactic intended to deceive the opposing side. These strategies helped gain strategic advantages in battles and contributed to the overall psychological warfare that characterized the conflict.

**World War II** saw an even more sophisticated use of propaganda and misinformation, with both **Nazi Germany** and the **Allied powers** employing extensive campaigns to influence public perception, boost morale, and demonize the enemy. Propaganda during this period became highly effective due to advances in mass communication technologies, such as radio, film, and mass-produced printed materials.

- **Nazi Germany**: Under the direction of **Joseph Goebbels**, the **Minister of Propaganda**, Nazi Germany used misinformation and propaganda extensively to promote its ideology and maintain control over the German population. The Nazi regime utilized **radio broadcasts, films, posters, and rallies** to create a narrative that portrayed Hitler as the savior of Germany, restoring the nation's honor and power. Propaganda also focused on promoting anti-Semitic views, with misinformation portraying **Jews** as the root cause of Germany's problems, from economic hardship to social unrest. The infamous propaganda film **"The Eternal Jew"** dehumanized Jewish people and framed them as a threat to German society. This widespread misinformation campaign played a crucial role in gaining public support for the regime's discriminatory policies and the **Holocaust**.
- **Allied Forces**: The **Allied powers**, including the United States, Britain, and the Soviet Union, also used propaganda to rally support for the war effort and demonize the Axis powers. In the United States, the **Office of War Information (OWI)** was responsible for disseminating propaganda through films, posters, and radio broadcasts. **Hollywood** played an essential role in producing films that depicted the war in a positive light, glorifying the sacrifices of American

soldiers while portraying the enemy as evil. The **"Why We Fight"** series, directed by Frank Capra, was created to educate American troops and the general public on the reasons behind the war, reinforcing the righteousness of the Allied cause and emphasizing the moral imperative of defeating fascism.

· **Misinformation to Boost Morale**: Allied propaganda often used **misleading narratives** to boost morale on the home front. The British government, for instance, downplayed the severity of the **Blitz**—the German bombing campaign on British cities—to prevent panic among the population. Positive stories about resilience and heroism were amplified to maintain a sense of unity and determination. In the Soviet Union, propaganda portrayed **Stalin** as a father figure and heroic leader, inspiring people to endure hardship and contribute to the war effort. Soviet propaganda also framed the conflict as the **"Great Patriotic War"**, emphasizing nationalism and the need to defend the motherland.

· **Demonizing the Enemy**: Both the Axis and Allied powers used propaganda to **demonize the enemy**. American and British propaganda depicted the Germans and Japanese as ruthless aggressors, often using racial stereotypes to dehumanize them. **Posters, cartoons, and films** frequently depicted Japanese soldiers in an exaggerated, inhuman manner, portraying them as a threat to American values and way of life. This type of propaganda fostered hatred and justified the war effort to the general public. The Japanese, in turn, used propaganda to frame the Western Allies as imperialist oppressors, portraying themselves as the liberators of Asia.

· **Operation Fortitude**: Misinformation was also used strategically by the Allies during military operations. A notable example is **Operation Fortitude**, part of the deception campaign leading up to the **D-Day invasion** in 1944. The Allies used fake radio transmissions, inflatable tanks, and double agents to convince the Germans that the invasion would take place at **Pas de Calais** rather than **Normandy**. This misinformation campaign successfully misled the German military, leading them to position their forces away from the actual invasion site, which contributed to the success of the D-Day landings.

· **Censorship and Control of Information**: Censorship was a crucial element of propaganda during World War II. Both Axis and Allied governments tightly controlled the information available to their populations. Newspapers, radio broadcasts, and other forms of media were censored to prevent the dissemination of information that could harm morale or lead to dissent. By controlling what information the public had access to, governments ensured that only a carefully curated version of the war reached the people— one that emphasized victories and minimized defeats.

In summary, during both **World War I** and **World War II**, **propaganda and misinformation** played a vital role in shaping public perception, boosting morale, and demonizing the enemy. Governments used a combination of exaggerated claims, emotionally charged imagery, and censorship to control the narrative and rally support for their causes. These efforts were instrumental in maintaining domestic unity and morale, influencing public opinion, and swaying the course of the wars. The extensive use of misinformation during these conflicts demonstrates how the manipulation of information can become a powerful tool in times of crisis, used to guide both individual beliefs and the broader course of history.

## 3.6 The Cold War Era: Information Warfare

The **Cold War**, spanning from the late 1940s to the early 1990s, was characterized by an ideological battle between the **Soviet Union** and the **United States**, with both sides employing **misinformation and propaganda** as essential tools in their quest for global influence. The use of misinformation during this period extended beyond military tactics, targeting **public opinion** at home and influencing allies and adversaries abroad. The Cold War saw the proliferation of **information warfare** as a critical dimension of geopolitical conflict, with each super-power attempting to portray itself as morally superior while discrediting the other.

- **Soviet Misinformation**: The Soviet Union used **propaganda** and misinformation extensively to control public perception within the country and discredit Western democracies. The Soviet leadership, through agencies such as **TASS** and **Pravda**, used media channels to paint the Soviet Union as a champion of the working class and an opponent of Western imperialism. Soviet propaganda depicted **capitalism** as a system that exploited workers and caused social inequalities, while communism was portrayed as a superior economic and social model that ensured equality and progress.
- **Disinformation campaigns**, known as **"active measures,"**

were also used to spread false narratives about the United States and its allies. One prominent example was **Operation INFEKTION**, a misinformation campaign orchestrated by the **KGB** in the 1980s, which falsely claimed that the **HIV/AIDS virus** had been created by the U.S. military as part of a biological warfare program. This story was disseminated through international media outlets and exploited the fears surrounding the HIV/AIDS crisis, leading to widespread mistrust of the United States globally.

- **American Misinformation**: In response, the United States used **psychological operations** (PSYOPs) to spread anti-communist messages both domestically and internationally. The **Voice of America** and **Radio Free Europe** were used to broadcast pro-Western content into Eastern Bloc countries, highlighting the benefits of capitalism, democracy, and personal freedoms while criticizing the oppressive nature of communist regimes. These broadcasts aimed to provide information that was restricted in communist countries, but they also contained exaggerated claims about life under capitalism and often omitted any negative aspects of Western policies.
- In addition to targeting audiences in the Eastern Bloc, American efforts were also directed at the domestic population. The U.S. government used **Hollywood films** as a medium for anti-communist propaganda, encouraging the production of movies that portrayed the Soviet Union as a menacing threat to freedom and democracy. Films like **"The Red Menace"** and **"Invasion of the Body Snatchers"** were designed to stoke fears about communism infiltrating American society, portraying communists as a hidden danger to the American way of life.

Both the Soviet and American misinformation efforts contributed to a climate of fear and distrust, which kept citizens on edge throughout the Cold War. The **narratives** crafted by both sides were designed to promote their respective ideologies and dehumanize the enemy, ensuring that the conflict remained not only a military and economic struggle but also a battle for the hearts and minds of people around the world.

**Case Study: The "Red Scare" in the United States:** A notable example of Cold War misinformation in the United States was the **"Red Scare"**—a period of intense fear of communism that led to widespread suspicion and the persecution of individuals believed to have communist ties. There were two major Red Scares in U.S. history, but the **second Red Scare** of the late 1940s and 1950s, led by **Senator Joseph McCarthy**, is particularly significant as a case study in the use of misinformation to create fear and control public perception.

During the second Red Scare, **Senator McCarthy** and others in the U.S. government claimed that communist spies had infiltrated the highest levels of American society, including the government, military, and entertainment industry. McCarthy's **House Un-American Activities Committee (HUAC)** hearings were used as a platform to accuse individuals of communist sympathies without substantial evidence. This led to numerous high-profile investigations, public interrogations, and blacklisting of people in various industries, particularly in Hollywood. Many people's careers and lives were ruined due to **unfounded accusations** and the climate of fear that resulted from McCarthy's allegations.

Misinformation played a crucial role in maintaining the **hysteria** surrounding the Red Scare. The American media, driven by sensationalism, often reported on alleged communist infiltration with little regard for accuracy. **Headlines** and news reports frequently exaggerated the extent of communist influence, contributing to a widespread belief that the country was on the brink of being overtaken by communists. This fear led to **paranoia**, where even slight associations with left-wing politics could result in individuals being labeled as a threat to national security.

The fear generated during the Red Scare was not solely due to McCarthy's efforts; it was also a product of Cold War-era propaganda that painted communism as an existential threat to American values. The U.S. government used **misinformation** to manipulate public opinion, cultivating a national sentiment of suspicion and conformity. Even as McCarthy's influence began to wane in the late 1950s, the damage had already been done—trust among citizens had eroded, and many had internalized the fear of an unseen communist menace.

The "Red Scare" is an important example of how **misinformation** can be used to control a population by fostering fear and paranoia. By spreading exaggerated or false claims about the threat of communism, American leaders were able to justify actions that limited civil liberties and reinforced political conformity. This misinformation campaign was aimed not just at countering communism abroad but also at ensuring that dissenting voices within the United States were silenced, thus maintaining a unified stance against the Soviet Union.

## 3.7 The Digital Age and the Shift in Misinformation Dynamics

The **advent of the internet** in the late 20th and early 21st centuries marked a significant turning point in how **misinformation** was disseminated and consumed. The rise of the internet opened up new pathways for the spread of information, bypassing traditional gatekeepers like publishers and broadcasters. This democratization of information allowed for greater freedom of expression and access to diverse viewpoints, but it also laid the groundwork for a new wave of **misinformation** and **disinformation** that would reshape public discourse.

In the **early 2000s**, **online forums** and **message boards** became breeding grounds for the rapid spread of **misinformation**. Websites like **4chan**, **Something Awful**, and various niche forums provided an unmoderated space where people could share information without much scrutiny. These platforms were often used to share conspiracy theories and exaggerated claims, which could spread unchecked and gain momentum. The absence of fact-checking mechanisms allowed false narratives to flourish, with users echoing each other's beliefs and amplifying misinformation in what essentially became **early echo chambers**. These forums facilitated the viral nature of false information, often starting small but eventually growing to influence larger groups.

One significant development during this period was the **rise of conspiracy theories** that gained traction through online communities. Conspiracy theories that once had limited reach were now finding large audiences. One notable example is the

**"9/11 truth movement"**, which emerged in the aftermath of the September 11, 2001, attacks. Online forums played a central role in spreading misinformation about the attacks, suggesting that they were an "inside job" orchestrated by the U.S. government. These claims, which lacked credible evidence, spread rapidly through forums, where like-minded individuals connected, reinforced each other's views, and created an online community that thrived on distrust of official narratives. The internet's reach allowed conspiracy theories to move from the fringes of society into mainstream discourse, setting the stage for a broader culture of misinformation.

During the **1990s and early 2000s**, **email chains** were a major vector for the spread of misinformation. As email became a popular form of communication, it also became a tool for spreading misleading stories, hoaxes, and conspiracy theories. These email chains often contained **alarmist content**, like claims about health risks, political scandals, or warnings about fabricated threats. The recipients of these emails—often well-meaning individuals—forwarded them to friends and family, unwittingly contributing to the spread of false information. Unlike more public forums, email chains were private and trusted, which made the misinformation they contained particularly insidious. People were more likely to believe and share content received from a trusted contact, reinforcing the misinformation cycle.

One classic example of misinformation spread through email chains involved **urban legends** and **false health advice**. Messages warning about common foods being poisonous, or claims about quick fixes for serious medical conditions, became widespread. The misinformation was often presented in a way that invoked fear, urgency, or authority, leading readers to accept the information without critically questioning its validity. This method of spreading misinformation laid the groundwork for future disinformation campaigns, as it became clear that content designed to evoke emotional responses could quickly go viral, even if the platform was as simple as an email inbox.

The **early internet forums** also contributed to the development of more advanced forms of **online manipulation**. Platforms like **Usenet** and **Yahoo! Groups** allowed individuals to form online communities based on shared interests, which included conspiracy theories, pseudoscience, and political misinformation. In these forums, users who might not have had any other avenue to express fringe beliefs were able to connect, share content, and validate each other's ideas. These online communities began to develop their own narratives, often diverging significantly from mainstream discourse. The **lack of moderation** and the anonymity of these forums made them ideal spaces for the development and spread of false information, as there were no accountability measures in place to prevent the spread of misleading or harmful narratives.

The use of **email chains and early online forums** in the 1990s and 2000s provided the foundation for what would eventually become the modern **social media misinformation landscape**. The mechanisms of misinformation—emotional manipulation, reliance on trust within personal networks, and the creation of echo chambers—remained largely the same, but the platforms evolved. As social media platforms like **Facebook** and **X** gained prominence, they inherited and amplified many of the issues first seen in email chains and forums, but on a much larger and more interconnected scale.

## 3.8 Conclusion

Throughout history, **manipulating information** has been a constant presence, evolving alongside advances in communication technologies. From **ancient rulers** spreading false narratives to maintain power, to **religious misinformation** during the medieval period, to **yellow journalism** and propaganda in the age of mass media, misinformation has always played a role in shaping public perception. Each new technological advance—from the **printing press** to the **radio** and beyond—has changed the way misinformation spreads, amplifying its reach and impact.

Understanding the **historical context** of misinformation is crucial for addressing the challenges we face today. By recognizing how misinformation has been used throughout history, we can better understand its mechanisms, anticipate its effects, and develop strategies to combat it. The lessons learned from the past inform our approach to safeguarding truth and ensuring that the spread of misinformation is effectively mitigated.

The next chapter will explore **media bias** on both the left and right and its role in influencing **American elections**, with a particular focus on the **upcoming 2024 elections**. Media bias has become a significant factor in shaping public perception, and understanding how different outlets present information is key to recognizing the broader effects of misinformation.

94

4

# Media Bias and the 2024 US Elections

**Media bias** plays a significant role in shaping public opinion, particularly during election cycles. By presenting information in a particular way, media outlets can influence how audiences perceive political candidates, policies, and events. **Media bias** refers to the tendency of news organizations to present stories and information in a manner that aligns with their ideological preferences or corporate interests. This bias can manifest in how stories are selected, framed, and reported, ultimately affecting how the public understands and responds to political developments.

**Media framing** is a crucial aspect of media bias, involving the way information is presented to shape the interpretation of events or issues. Framing can determine the **salience** of particular topics and how they are understood by the audience. For instance, a news outlet might focus heavily on a candidate's mistakes or controversial comments, thereby framing them as incompetent or untrustworthy. Conversely, positive framing, such as emphasizing a candidate's achievements and personal qualities, can create a favorable perception. The impact of media framing on **voter perceptions** is substantial, as it can influence opinions, reinforce biases, and shape the decision-making process. When voters are repeatedly exposed to certain narratives or frames, they are more likely to adopt those viewpoints as their own, even when presented with contradictory information.

In the **2024 US elections cycle**, media bias has been especially significant due to the heightened **polarization** of both the electorate and media outlets. News organizations, ranging from traditional television networks to digital and social media platforms, have become increasingly divided along ideological lines. As a result, audiences are more likely to receive information that confirms their existing beliefs, rather than being exposed to a balanced perspective. The **partisan nature** of media coverage has contributed to increased polarization, making it more challenging for voters to discern objective truths about candidates and their platforms.

The **upcoming 2024 election** is also unique in terms of the role that social media will play in disseminating information and potentially amplifying media bias. Social media platforms like **X, Facebook, and TikTok** serve as primary news sources for many voters, with their algorithms designed to promote content that aligns with users' preferences. This algorithm-driven content curation creates **filter bubbles** that reinforce pre-existing beliefs and contribute to a biased information environment. The result is that voters are more likely to be exposed to partisan content that shapes their perceptions of candidates, issues, and the election as a whole.

Media bias in the context of the 2024 elections is not limited to traditional news outlets but extends to **influencers**, **podcasts**, and even **satirical shows** that engage audiences in political discourse. The influence of these non-traditional media sources further complicates the landscape of election coverage, making it imperative for voters to approach information critically and seek out diverse perspectives. As media bias continues to shape voter attitudes and behaviors, understanding its mechanisms and recognizing its effects is crucial for safeguarding an informed and engaged electorate.

## 4.1 Understanding Media Bias

**Media bias** refers to the tendency of news organizations to report events and issues in a manner that reflects their own perspectives or interests, rather than offering an impartial or balanced view. It affects how stories are covered, the emphasis placed on certain topics, and the language used in reporting. Media bias can take various forms, including:

- **Selection Bias**: This form of bias occurs when media outlets choose which stories to report on and which to ignore. Selection bias determines the **agenda**—what audiences will hear about and what will be excluded from public discourse. By selectively covering certain events, media outlets shape what the public perceives as important. For example, a news outlet might prioritize coverage of specific protests while ignoring others, influencing the audience's perception of which issues are most pressing.
- **Framing Bias**: **Framing** involves presenting a story in a particular way to emphasize certain aspects over others. By framing events in a specific context, media outlets can

influence how those events are understood. For instance, reporting on immigration could be framed as a humanitarian crisis or as a security threat, depending on the outlet's ideological leaning. The chosen frame determines how audiences interpret the underlying issues, often leading to differing conclusions about the same set of facts.

- **Sensationalism**: Sensationalism involves emphasizing dramatic, shocking, or emotionally charged aspects of a story to capture attention. This type of bias is often motivated by a desire for higher ratings or clicks. Headlines and stories are exaggerated or focus on conflict to generate **emotional reactions**, leading to a skewed understanding of the issue. Sensational coverage of political disputes, for instance, often creates the impression of extreme division, even in situations where common ground exists.

**Traditional media**—such as **television networks** and **newspapers**—and **new media**—including **social media platforms** and **digital news outlets**—are both affected by media bias, but the ways in which they manifest differ. In traditional media, bias can be seen in the selection of experts or sources, the editorial decisions that guide story placement, and even the language used in reporting. For example, some networks may give significantly more airtime to a political candidate whose views align with their audience's preferences, while others may focus more on the candidate's shortcomings.

In **new media**, media bias is further complicated by the influence of **algorithms** that determine which content is most visible. Social media platforms like **Facebook** and **X** use algorithms designed to maximize engagement, which often means promoting content that evokes strong emotional responses—

frequently, content that is biased or sensational. These algorithms create **filter bubbles**, in which users are exposed primarily to information that aligns with their existing beliefs, reinforcing bias and further polarizing public opinion. For example, a conservative user might see more news stories from right-leaning outlets, while a liberal user is exposed to more left-leaning content, leading to divergent views on the same issues.

Media bias can be found across the political spectrum, with **left-leaning** and **right-leaning** outlets both framing news stories in ways that align with their respective ideologies. Left-leaning media outlets, such as **MSNBC** or **The New York Times**, tend to emphasize social justice issues, environmental concerns, and critiques of conservative policies. For example, left-leaning coverage of healthcare debates may frame universal healthcare as a fundamental right, focusing on personal stories of individuals struggling without adequate coverage.

Conversely, **right-leaning** media outlets, such as **Fox News** or **The Daily Caller**, tend to emphasize issues like national security, law and order, and economic freedom. In covering the same healthcare debate, these outlets might focus on the potential economic burdens of government-run healthcare or highlight concerns about increased taxes and government overreach.

These differing narratives influence how audiences perceive the **2024 US elections**, with left-leaning outlets generally providing more critical coverage of conservative candidates, while right-leaning outlets emphasize flaws in liberal policies and candidates. As a result, viewers of these media sources are likely to develop perspectives that align with the biases presented, contributing to political polarization.

The presence of **media bias** across traditional and digital platforms significantly impacts voter perceptions, often making it difficult for individuals to access balanced information. This reality highlights the importance of **media literacy** and the need for consumers to critically evaluate news content by seeking diverse sources and being aware of potential biases.

## 4.2 Historical Context of Media Bias in US Elections

**Media bias** has played a significant role in shaping public perception and influencing voter behavior throughout the history of **US elections**. Examining past elections reveals how different media outlets have used their platforms to sway public sentiment, either intentionally or inadvertently. The role of media bias in the electoral process has evolved significantly over time, from the dominance of print media to the rise of broadcast television, and now the prevalence of digital and social media.

### 4.2.1 Past US Elections and Media Bias

In the **2000 presidential election** between **George W. Bush** and **Al Gore**, media coverage was highly influential in shaping voter perceptions of both candidates, particularly during the chaotic aftermath of Election Day. The role of the media in declaring **winners** in key states before all votes were counted was particularly contentious. For example, on election night, major news networks initially declared Gore the winner in **Florida**, only to retract the call later and then declare Bush the winner. This premature and contradictory reporting led to widespread confusion among voters and contributed to the sense of distrust and controversy surrounding the recount process. The extensive media focus on the **Florida recount** highlighted the power of media narratives in influencing public perception, with many outlets framing the recount as a partisan battle rather than a necessary democratic process.

The **2016 presidential election** between **Donald Trump** and **Hillary Clinton** further highlighted the influence of media bias. During this election, **left-leaning** media outlets like **CNN** and **The New York Times** were often accused of favoring Clinton, focusing on her qualifications and portraying her as the more experienced candidate. In contrast, **right-leaning** media outlets like **Fox News** and **Breitbart** framed Trump as an outsider challenging the political establishment. Media bias was evident in the coverage of key events, such as the handling of **Clinton's email scandal** and the portrayal of Trump's **"Make America Great Again"** campaign. The way these stories were framed significantly influenced voter sentiment, contributing to the **polarization** of the electorate. Additionally, the rise of **social media** and the prevalence of **fake news** during the 2016 campaign further complicated the media landscape, with misinformation spreading rapidly and contributing to an environment of distrust.

The **2020 presidential election** between **Donald Trump** and **Joe Biden** was another significant example of media bias's impact on voter sentiment. The **COVID-19 pandemic** and issues surrounding **mail-in voting** became central themes in media coverage, with left-leaning outlets emphasizing the importance of mail-in ballots for public safety and right-leaning outlets focusing on potential **voter fraud**. The coverage of the pandemic also reflected clear biases, as left-leaning media outlets highlighted Trump's perceived mishandling of the crisis, while right-leaning outlets framed the pandemic response as an overreach by government officials and an attack on personal freedoms. The result was a highly polarized media environment in which voters were exposed primarily to information that aligned with their existing beliefs, reinforcing divisions and shaping perceptions of the election's legitimacy.

## 4.2.2 Evolution of Partisan Media and Increasing Polarization

The evolution of **partisan media** in the United States has contributed significantly to the **increasing polarization** of news coverage over the past several decades. In the early days of American democracy, newspapers were explicitly partisan, often funded by political parties to promote their agendas. As the media landscape evolved, particularly in the 20th century, there was a shift towards more **objective journalism**, with major networks like **CBS, NBC, and ABC** striving for neutrality in their coverage. However, with the advent of **cable news** in the 1980s and the rise of **24-hour news cycles**, networks began to differentiate themselves by catering to specific audience demographics, leading to a resurgence of partisan reporting.

The launch of **Fox News** in 1996 marked a turning point in the evolution of partisan media. Fox News presented itself as an alternative to what it perceived as a **liberal bias** in mainstream media, appealing to conservative audiences. This shift prompted the rise of explicitly partisan news networks, with **MSNBC** emerging as a counterbalance to Fox, catering to more liberal viewers. The increasing polarization of cable news networks created an environment in which viewers could choose to consume news that aligned with their political beliefs, rather than seeking out balanced perspectives.

The rise of **digital media** and **social media platforms** in the 21st century further exacerbated media bias and polarization. Social media algorithms, designed to maximize engagement, often promote content that aligns with users' pre-existing beliefs, creating **filter bubbles** that limit exposure to diverse viewpoints. This phenomenon has contributed to the deepening divide in how Americans understand and interpret political events, as voters are increasingly exposed only to narratives that reinforce their biases. Platforms like **Facebook** and **X** have become significant players in the dissemination of news, with both traditional media outlets and independent content creators using these platforms to reach audiences. The result is a fragmented media landscape in which partisan perspectives dominate, and misinformation can spread unchecked.

In summary, the **historical context of media bias in US elections** reveals a clear pattern of evolving influence, from the partisan press of the early republic to the increasingly polarized digital landscape of today. The role of media in shaping voter sentiment has only grown more complex with each election cycle, highlighting the need for media literacy and critical thinking as voters navigate a media environment that is often more focused on reinforcing ideological narratives than providing objective information.

## 4.3 Media Bias on the Left

**Media bias** in left-leaning outlets often manifests in how stories are selected, framed, and presented to the public, with a focus on issues that align with **progressive** values such as social justice, economic equality, and environmental protection. These outlets typically emphasize systemic inequalities, portray liberal policies in a favorable light, and scrutinize conservative actions more heavily. This approach shapes the narrative presented to audiences, reinforcing a particular worldview that resonates with liberal voters.

**Left-leaning media outlets**, such as **CNN, MSNBC, The New York Times**, and **The Washington Post**, often present news with a focus on progressive and liberal perspectives. This can be seen in the choice of topics covered, the language used, and the framing of key political issues. For instance, coverage of **social justice** topics, such as racial inequality, LGBTQ+ rights, and gender equity, tends to be more prevalent and framed in ways that highlight the need for government intervention and reform.

One form of bias often seen in left-leaning outlets is **selection bias**, where certain stories are prioritized over others to emphasize issues important to the liberal base. For example, these outlets may give extensive coverage to topics such as **climate change**, focusing on the urgency of addressing environmental concerns and highlighting the shortcomings of conservative policies on the matter. This emphasis aligns with the broader liberal agenda of pushing for stronger environmental protections and government action to combat climate change.

**Framing bias** is also common, where stories are presented in a way that emphasizes certain aspects while downplaying others. For instance, left-leaning outlets might frame **universal healthcare** as a moral imperative, focusing on the positive impacts it could have on marginalized communities and downplaying concerns about costs or potential downsides. This framing helps to build support for policies favored by progressive lawmakers and positions opposition to such policies as morally questionable.

Another element of media bias in these outlets is **sensationalism**, particularly when covering controversial actions or statements by conservative figures. Left-leaning outlets may highlight scandals or missteps by conservative politicians, using sensational headlines to generate outrage among their audience. This approach not only drives viewership but also reinforces negative perceptions of conservative leaders among liberal viewers.

## 4.3.1 Examples of Left-Leaning Media Coverage in the 2024 Election

In the **2024 election cycle**, left-leaning media outlets have continued to play a significant role in shaping public perception of the candidates and key issues. For example, **CNN** and **MSNBC** have provided extensive coverage of **reproductive rights** and **abortion access**, often highlighting the differences between Democratic and Republican approaches. Coverage has frequently emphasized the Democratic commitment to protecting and expanding abortion rights, while portraying the Republican stance as restrictive and out of touch with public opinion on reproductive health. Retrieved from: https://www

.pewresearch.org/politics/2024/06/06/cultural-issues-and-the-2024-election/

Another example can be seen in the coverage of **voting rights**. **The New York Times** has highlighted Republican efforts to implement stricter voting laws, framing them as attempts to suppress voter turnout, particularly among minority communities. This coverage has focused on the negative implications of these laws, painting them as threats to democracy and disproportionately affecting marginalized groups. By framing the issue in this way, left-leaning outlets aim to rally their audience around the need for federal voting protections and increase support for Democratic-led initiatives to expand voter access. Retrieved from: https://www.nytimes.com/topic/subje ct/voting-rights-registration-and-requirements

The coverage of **economic inequality** is another area where left-leaning media bias is evident. Outlets like **The Washington Post** have frequently run stories on the growing wealth gap and the need for progressive taxation to address income inequality. These stories often highlight the success of Democratic candidates in advocating for policies that benefit the middle and working classes, such as increased minimum wages and expanded social safety nets. In contrast, Republican economic policies are often portrayed as favoring the wealthy, contributing to an unfair system that perpetuates inequality. Retrieved from: https://www.washingtonpost.com/opinions/2024/01/ 25/economic-inequality-despair-redistribution/

## 4.3.2 Influence on Liberal Voters

The influence of left-leaning media outlets on **liberal voters** is significant, as the framing of stories and the choice of topics covered serve to reinforce existing beliefs and align with progressive values. By focusing on issues such as **reproductive rights, social justice, healthcare reform, and climate change**, left-leaning media helps to shape the priorities of liberal voters, often framing these issues as urgent crises that require immediate action. This approach not only informs liberal voters but also motivates them to support candidates who align with these priorities.

The use of **emotional appeals** in reporting is another way in which left-leaning media outlets influence their audience. Stories about **abortion, healthcare struggles**, **racial injustice**, or **environmental disasters** are often framed in a way that elicits empathy and a sense of urgency, encouraging viewers to advocate for change. By presenting these issues in a highly personal and emotional context, left-leaning media outlets are able to build strong support for progressive policies among their audience.

The **confirmation bias** effect is also at play, as liberal viewers are more likely to consume media that aligns with their existing beliefs. Left-leaning media outlets cater to this audience by presenting stories that validate their worldview, creating a feedback loop that reinforces liberal perspectives and strengthens support for Democratic candidates. This selective exposure to information contributes to **political polarization**, as viewers are less likely to encounter opposing viewpoints or consider alternative interpretations of events.

## 4.4 Media Bias on the Right

**Media bias** in **right-leaning outlets** often manifests through selective coverage, framing, and sensationalism that aligns with **conservative values** such as limited government, individual liberties, national security, and traditional social norms. Right-leaning media outlets typically emphasize stories that criticize liberal policies, promote conservative ideals, and present Democratic candidates in a negative light. This kind of biased reporting shapes the narrative for audiences, reinforcing conservative viewpoints and highlighting issues that resonate with right-leaning voters.

Right-leaning outlets, such as **Fox News**, **The Daily Caller**, and **Breitbart**, provide news coverage that reflects conservative perspectives. This is evident in the topics covered, the framing of issues, and the language used to present information. **Selection bias** is a notable form of bias, where these outlets often choose to cover issues that align with their audience's preferences, such as **border security**, **law and order**, and **economic freedom**. These topics are typically framed to highlight the failures of liberal policies and to support a conservative approach to governance.

**Framing bias** is also prevalent, with right-leaning media often framing issues in a way that aligns with conservative values. For example, coverage of government programs and welfare initiatives might focus on the costs and inefficiencies of these programs, portraying them as a burden on taxpayers. Conversely, coverage of tax cuts is framed positively, emphasizing the benefits for businesses and economic growth. The use of specific language, such as referring to undocumented immigrants as **"illegal aliens"**, is also a form of framing that influences how audiences perceive these individuals and the broader issue of immigration. Retrieved from: https://www.researchgate.net/publication/316520230_Framing_immigrants_News_coverage_public_opinion_and_policy

**Sensationalism** is another aspect of media bias in right-leaning outlets, particularly when covering actions or statements by liberal figures. Right-leaning outlets often use **sensational headlines** to emphasize scandals or controversies involving Democratic politicians. This approach not only draws in viewers but also reinforces negative perceptions of liberal leaders and their policies among conservative audiences.

## 4.4.1 Examples of Right-Leaning Media Coverage in the 2024 Election

In the **2024 election**, right-leaning media outlets have played a significant role in shaping the narrative around the candidates and key issues. For example, **Fox News** has extensively covered **border security**, focusing on the Republican commitment to strengthening the southern border and portraying Democratic candidates as weak on immigration. This coverage has emphasized the risks of illegal immigration, including concerns about **crime** and **drug trafficking**, while framing Republican candidates as the best option for ensuring national security and protecting American jobs. Retrieved from: https://www.foxnews.com/us/whistleblowers-border-patrol-surveillance-cameras-out-service-gop-demands-answers-dhs

Another example can be seen in the coverage of **economic**

**policies**. Right-leaning outlets such as **The Daily Caller** have highlighted **taxation** and the impact of government spending, framing Democratic proposals for increased taxes on the wealthy as harmful to economic growth and small businesses. This coverage has focused on portraying Democratic economic policies as **socialist** and burdensome, while presenting Republican policies as promoting **free-market principles** and benefiting the middle class by reducing taxes and regulations. Retrieved from:

Fox News. (2024). *Whistleblowers Claim Border Patrol Surveillance Cameras Are Out of Service; GOP Demands Answers from DHS.* Retrieved from https://dailycaller.com/2024/10/16/environm ental-justice-advisors-raked-500-million-taxpayers/

During the 2024 election cycle, **Breitbart** has provided significant coverage of **culture war issues**, including debates over **gender identity** and **school curriculums**. Stories have often highlighted instances where Democratic policies or progressive social movements are portrayed as overreaching or infringing on individual freedoms, such as parental rights in education. This framing resonates with conservative voters, who are often concerned about perceived government overreach and the influence of progressive ideologies on traditional values. Retrieved from: https://www.breitbart.com/politics/2024/10/ 16/just-ban-it-donald-trump-vows-executive-action-keep- men-off-female-sports-teams/

## 4.4.2 Influence on Conservative Voters

The influence of right-leaning media outlets on **conservative voters** is substantial, as these outlets shape how key issues are understood and prioritized. By focusing on topics like **border security, law enforcement, and tax cuts**, right-leaning media reinforces the idea that conservative policies are best suited to address the country's challenges. This kind of coverage helps solidify conservative voters' support for Republican candidates, as it presents them as defenders of national security, personal freedoms, and economic prosperity.

The use of **emotional appeals** is also a critical element of right-leaning media bias. By highlighting stories that evoke fear or anger—such as coverage of rising crime rates or government regulations—these outlets tap into the emotions of their audience, creating a sense of urgency around issues that align with conservative values. This emotional framing can motivate conservative voters to support Republican candidates who promise to address these concerns.

**Confirmation bias** plays a significant role in the relationship between right-leaning media and its audience. Conservative viewers are more likely to consume news that aligns with their existing beliefs, and right-leaning media outlets cater to this preference by providing stories that validate their audience's worldview. This creates a **feedback loop**, where viewers are repeatedly exposed to information that reinforces their political preferences, making them less likely to consider alternative viewpoints or engage with opposing perspectives.

Right-leaning media outlets also contribute to **political polarization** by portraying liberal policies and Democratic candidates in a consistently negative light. This type of coverage can deepen divisions between conservative and liberal voters, as it reinforces negative stereotypes and frames political opponents as threats to American values and freedoms. By presenting a one-sided narrative, right-leaning media outlets encourage their audience to view political issues through a partisan lens, ultimately contributing to the broader polarization of the electorate.

## 4.5 Polling, and Its Influence on Elections

**Polling** plays a significant role in modern elections, serving as a tool for both media outlets and political campaigns to gauge public sentiment and predict election outcomes. Polls are conducted by a variety of organizations, including **media companies**, **academic institutions**, and **independent pollsters**, each with their own methodologies and potential biases. While polling can provide valuable insights into voter preferences and trends, it can also be used to shape public perception and influence voter behavior—sometimes in misleading ways.

### 4.5.1 Correct and Incorrect Uses of Polls

Polls can be used **correctly** when they are conducted with **representative sampling, transparent methodologies**, and **unbiased questions**. When polling organizations adhere to best practices, they can provide an accurate reflection of public opinion, allowing campaigns to understand voter preferences and adjust their strategies accordingly. Accurate polling also informs the public and can help voters understand where candidates stand on key issues.

However, polls can also be used **incorrectly**, often as a tool for **influencing public opinion** rather than merely measuring it. **Push polling**, for example, is a technique in which a poll is used to sway voters by presenting biased or leading questions. These polls are designed to produce results that align with a particular narrative or agenda, rather than genuinely gauging public sentiment. Additionally, **media outlets** may selectively report on polling data that supports their preferred candidate or ideology, while ignoring polls that present contradictory results. This selective reporting can create a false sense of momentum for a candidate, potentially influencing voter turnout and fundraising efforts.

## 4.5.2 Polling Bias and Its Implications

Like media coverage, polls can also be subject to various forms of **bias** that impact their accuracy and reliability. Some of the common types of polling biases include:

- **Selection Bias**: Selection bias occurs when the sample of respondents does not accurately represent the broader population. For instance, if a poll relies too heavily on responses from one demographic—such as older voters or urban residents—the results may not accurately reflect the preferences of the entire electorate. This type of bias can skew the results and create a misleading picture of voter sentiment.

- **Question Framing Bias**: The way questions are worded in a poll can significantly affect the responses. Pollsters may use loaded or leading language to elicit a particular answer, which can create a **framing bias**. For example, asking voters whether they support a "tax relief plan" versus a "tax cut for the wealthy" can produce different results, even if both questions refer to the same policy.
- **Non-Response Bias**: **Non-response bias** occurs when certain groups of people are less likely to respond to polls, which can distort the results. For example, younger voters or minority groups may be underrepresented in polling data if they are less likely to answer survey calls or participate in online polls. This can lead to inaccurate predictions about election outcomes, particularly if these underrepresented groups turn out in large numbers on Election Day.

In the **2024 election cycle**, polling bias has already played a role in shaping narratives around candidate viability and voter enthusiasm. For example, some polls conducted early in the campaign season have been criticized for underrepresenting certain demographics, such as young voters and ethnic minorities, leading to predictions that may not fully capture the diverse electorate. Additionally, media outlets have used early polling results to declare certain candidates as "frontrunners" or "long shots," which can create a **self-fulfilling prophecy**—voters may be more inclined to support a candidate who appears to have a strong chance of winning, while abandoning those perceived as having little chance of success. Retrieved from: https://projects.fivethirtyeight.com/polls/

## 4.5.3 Kamala Harris and Polling Influence

Polling data has shown **Kamala Harris** maintaining a strong lead among key demographics, such as young voters, women, and ethnic minorities. Media outlets like **CNN** and **MSNBC** have frequently highlighted these polling numbers to emphasize her broad appeal among diverse groups, framing her as a candidate capable of uniting various segments of the electorate. This positive polling coverage has helped Harris maintain an image of electability and momentum, which has been crucial in attracting campaign donations and endorsements.

However, polling has also highlighted challenges for Harris, particularly among independent voters and those concerned with economic issues. Right-leaning outlets such as **Fox News** have used these polling figures to frame Harris as a candidate struggling to gain support beyond the Democratic base, suggesting that her policies may not resonate with moderate or swing voters. This kind of framing can influence voter perceptions by creating doubt about her ability to appeal to a broader electorate.

## 4.5.4 Donald Trump and Polling Influence

Polling data for **Donald Trump** has been equally influential in shaping his campaign narrative. Trump has maintained strong polling numbers among his core supporters, particularly among rural voters, conservatives, and those who feel disillusioned with the current administration. Right-leaning media outlets like **Fox News** and **Breitbart** have frequently highlighted these polling numbers, framing Trump as the candidate of choice for those who want to challenge the status quo and restore a sense of traditional American values.

On the other hand, left-leaning media outlets have focused on polls that show Trump's unfavorable ratings among key demographics, such as women and young voters. Outlets like The New York Times have used these figures to question Trump's electability, particularly in a general election scenario where broad appeal is necessary. This focus on unfavorable polling data can shape public perception by portraying Trump as a divisive figure who may struggle to secure enough votes to win the election.

## 4.5.5 Polling and Fundraising

Polling and **fundraising** are closely linked in modern elections, as polling results can have a significant impact on a candidate's ability to raise money. When a candidate performs well in the polls, it can generate positive media coverage, boost donor confidence, and lead to an influx of campaign contributions. Conversely, poor polling results can lead to a drop in donations, as potential donors may perceive a candidate as unlikely to win and therefore not worth supporting.

Candidates and political action committees (PACs) often use polling data to target their fundraising efforts. For example, a candidate who is polling well in a particular state may focus fundraising efforts there to capitalize on perceived momentum. Conversely, if polling indicates that a candidate is struggling in a specific demographic, fundraising messages may be tailored to appeal to that group in an effort to improve polling numbers.

The influence of polling on fundraising also extends to **media coverage**. Media outlets often focus on polling data when discussing a candidate's viability, and candidates who are polling well are more likely to receive positive coverage. This creates a cycle in which strong polling leads to increased media attention, which in turn leads to more donations, further boosting the candidate's chances. On the other hand, candidates who poll poorly may struggle to gain traction, as they receive less media coverage and fewer donations, making it difficult to improve their standing in subsequent polls.

## 4.5.6 The Impact on Voter Behavior

Polling can also influence **voter behavior** in several ways. The **bandwagon effect** refers to the tendency of voters to support a candidate who appears to be leading in the polls, as people are often drawn to winners. This can create an artificial boost in support for a candidate who is perceived as having momentum, regardless of their actual qualifications or policies. Conversely, the **underdog effect** occurs when voters rally behind a candidate who is trailing in the polls, often out of sympathy or a desire to see an upset.

The impact of polling on voter behavior is particularly pronounced in **primary elections**, where voters may use polling data to decide which candidate to support based on perceived electability. In the **2024 election cycle**, polling data has been a key factor in shaping the narratives around various candidates, with media outlets frequently discussing candidates' standings in the polls and their chances of winning the nomination. This emphasis on polling can lead to a focus on **electability** rather than on the candidates' policies or qualifications, ultimately shaping the choices voters make at the ballot box.

## 4.6 Social Media and Algorithms

**Social media platforms** play a significant role in **perpetuating media bias** by amplifying certain types of content and limiting exposure to diverse viewpoints. Platforms like **Facebook**, **X (formerly Twitter)**, and **TikTok** are driven by algorithms designed to maximize user engagement. These algorithms determine what content users see, often favoring sensational or emotionally charged posts that are likely to generate clicks, shares, and comments. As a result, users are more likely to encounter content that aligns with their pre-existing beliefs, reinforcing biases and creating an echo chamber effect.

### 4.6.1 The Role of Algorithms in Creating Filter Bubbles

**Algorithms** are the driving force behind the content curation on social media platforms. They use data from users' past behavior—such as the posts they like, share, and comment on—to tailor their feeds to show more of the same type of content. This personalized content curation can lead to the creation of **filter bubbles**, in which users are predominantly exposed to information that supports their existing views. This reinforcement of pre-existing beliefs can contribute to **political polarization**, as individuals become more entrenched in their viewpoints and less open to alternative perspectives.

For example, if a user frequently interacts with conservative content, the platform's algorithm will prioritize similar content, effectively creating an environment where the user is exposed primarily to conservative viewpoints. The same is true for liberal content. This selective exposure limits users' ability to engage with diverse perspectives, making it more difficult to have a well-rounded understanding of political issues. The **filter bubble** effect contributes to the growing divide between political groups, as users are less likely to encounter content that challenges their views or encourages critical thinking.

## 4.6.2 Spread of Misinformation and Partisan Content in the 2024 Election Cycle

The **2024 election cycle** has been marked by the rapid spread of **misinformation** and **partisan content** on social media platforms, with algorithms playing a key role in amplifying these narratives. During this election cycle, platforms like Facebook, X, and TikTok have been used to spread misleading information about candidates, voting procedures, and key political issues. The algorithms on these platforms often prioritize content that evokes strong emotional reactions, such as anger or fear, which has led to the widespread dissemination of false and misleading information.

On **Facebook**, misinformation about voting procedures, such as incorrect dates or requirements for mail-in ballots, has been shared extensively in politically homogeneous groups. These groups, often consisting of individuals with similar political beliefs, serve as echo chambers where misinformation is less likely to be challenged. Facebook's algorithm, which prioritizes content that receives high engagement, has inadvertently amplified these false narratives, contributing to confusion among voters about the electoral process. Retrieved from: https://www.cnbc.com/2024/09/26/facebooks-misinformation-problem-has-local-election-officials-on-edge.html

**X** has also been a significant platform for the spread of partisan content during the 2024 election. Politicians, influencers, and users have used the platform to share misleading information about opponents and amplify polarizing narratives. The algorithm on X favors content that generates engagement, such as retweets and likes, which means that sensational and emotionally charged posts are more likely to gain traction. For instance, a misleading post about a candidate's stance on a controversial issue can quickly go viral, influencing public perception before fact-checkers have a chance to intervene.

On **TikTok**, the spread of misinformation has been particularly problematic among younger voters. TikTok's algorithm, which is designed to keep users engaged by showing them content similar to what they have previously interacted with, has led to the rapid spread of partisan and misleading videos. In the 2024 election cycle, videos containing false information about candidates' policies and personal lives have gone viral, reaching millions of users in a short period of time. These videos often use humor, music, and visual effects to make the content more engaging, making it difficult for viewers to discern fact from fiction.

The impact of these **filter bubbles** and the spread of misinformation on social media during the 2024 election cycle highlights the challenges of maintaining an informed electorate in the digital age. Social media platforms, driven by algorithms that prioritize engagement over accuracy, have become fertile ground for the spread of false information and partisan content. This has significant implications for the democratic process, as voters are making decisions based on incomplete or inaccurate information.

## 4.7 The Impact of Media Bias on Voter Behavior

Media bias can have a profound influence on voter behavior, significantly shaping the perceptions and attitudes of the electorate. This influence can manifest in several ways:

- **Shaping Voter Perceptions**: Biased media coverage often frames political issues in a particular light, leading to an uneven portrayal of candidates and their policies. This skewed presentation can enhance the appeal of one candidate while discrediting others, thereby impacting how voters perceive candidates and make decisions. For instance, favorable coverage of a candidate by major media outlets can give an impression of credibility and popularity, leading to increased support, while negative or dismissive coverage of other candidates can discourage voters from supporting them. A notable example is the 2016 U.S. Presidential election, where certain media outlets were criticized for giving disproportionately negative coverage to one candidate, thus swaying public opinion.

- **Affecting Voter Turnout**: Media bias can also influence voter turnout. When a candidate is portrayed as being significantly ahead, it can lead to voter complacency among their supporters, reducing the perceived urgency to vote. Conversely, it can also discourage voters of the other candidate, leading them to believe their participation is futile. This phenomenon is closely tied to the "bandwagon effect," where voters tend to support the candidate they believe is likely to win, based on media narratives. For more insight, a study published in the *American Political Science Review* showed that repeated exposure to biased political reporting can either encourage or suppress voter turnout, depending on how the coverage aligns with the voter's existing beliefs.

## 4.7.1 The Role of Confirmation Bias in Consuming Media Content and Its Impact on Political Polarization

Confirmation bias is a critical factor in how individuals consume media. People are naturally inclined to seek information that aligns with their pre-existing beliefs and to reject information that contradicts them. This leads to the creation of echo chambers, where individuals are only exposed to information that reinforces their views. Such environments amplify political polarization, deepening divides and reducing the potential for meaningful cross-party dialogue.

· **Media Echo Chambers and Polarization**: Social media algorithms tend to show users content similar to what they have previously engaged with, creating a feedback loop that reinforces beliefs without challenging them. This contributes to extreme partisanship and reduces the ability to see issues from other perspectives. For instance, a study by the *Pew Research Center* revealed that politically engaged individuals are more likely to follow news sources that reflect their political leanings, which in turn increases polarization.

## 4.7.2 The Potential Consequences of Biased Reporting on Public Trust in the Electoral Process

The credibility of the electoral process relies heavily on public trust, and biased reporting can undermine this trust. When voters perceive media as biased, they may believe that elections are inherently unfair or rigged, which can delegitimize the results. This is particularly problematic in close elections, where accusations of bias can fuel claims of voter fraud or systemic manipulation, leading to public distrust.

· **Erosion of Trust**: When voters lose confidence in the fairness of the media and perceive it as a mouthpiece for particular interests, they may also lose trust in democratic institutions. This has been observed in the United States, where increasing mistrust in media has correlated with declining public trust in government. A report from the

*Reuters Institute for the Study of Journalism* noted that public trust in media was significantly lower in countries with high levels of perceived media bias, which has implications for trust in broader societal institutions. Retrieved from: https://reutersinstitute.politics.ox.ac.uk/digital-news-re port/2024/public-perspectives-trust-news

## 4.8 Media Bias and Voter Perceptions

Media bias plays a significant role in shaping voter perceptions, often creating a skewed image of candidates and their policies. For example, biased media coverage may disproportionately present the achievements of one candidate while amplifying the negative aspects of another, thereby influencing voters' opinions and decision-making. This effect can ultimately impact election outcomes by altering voter expectations and preferences. According to a study, voter perception is influenced by the media's portrayal of candidates, with biased reporting potentially shaping voters' understanding of key issues and political dynamics. Retrieved from: https://journals .sagepub.com/doi/10.1177/13540688231187964

## 4.8.1 Media Bias and Voter Turnout

Media bias can also have a significant effect on voter turnout. Coverage that suggests a particular candidate is sure to win may lead to complacency among supporters or discourage opponents from participating, believing their vote won't make a difference. This phenomenon, often termed the "bandwagon effect," can either mobilize or suppress voter turnout based on perceived outcomes. The EAC report on election security further emphasizes that biased narratives in media can lead to a lack of trust in the fairness of the process, discouraging voters from participating altogether. Retrieved from: https://www.eac.gov/voters/election-security

## 4.8.2 Confirmation Bias and Political Polarization

Confirmation bias, the tendency for individuals to favor information that confirms their pre-existing beliefs, exacerbates political polarization. People tend to consume media content that aligns with their views, leading to the creation of echo chambers. This can significantly reduce exposure to opposing perspectives and contribute to further polarization within the electorate. The U.S. Department of Education highlights this issue in its Voter Toolkit, explaining that educational institutions can play a critical role in providing balanced civic education to counteract confirmation bias and encourage informed decision-making. Retrieved from: https://civilrights.org/2024/02/26/doe-voter-registration-toolkit/

### 4.8.3 Public Trust in the Electoral Process

The potential consequences of biased reporting on public trust in the electoral process are profound. When media outlets are perceived as serving partisan interests rather than presenting objective information, public trust in the electoral system is undermined. The CISA report on election security underlines the risks of media bias leading to misinformation and ultimately eroding confidence in the integrity of the electoral process. The report suggests that fair and transparent reporting is crucial for maintaining the legitimacy of elections and ensuring voter confidence. Retrieved from: https://www.cisa.gov/topics/election-security

## 4.9 Strategies for Identifying and Mitigating Media Bias

To address media bias as a consumer, it is essential to develop strategies for identifying and mitigating biases in news consumption:

- **Use Media Bias Charts Cautiously**: Tools like the AllSides Media Bias Chart help categorize news sources across the political spectrum, but over-reliance can be problematic, as these ratings are inherently limited. Instead, use such charts as a starting point to understand general leanings and supplement them with further critical analysis of individual articles and sources. AllSides and Ad Fontes Media both provide methodologies that are useful for understanding bias but require cautious interpretation (POYNTER). Retrieved from: https://www.poynter.org/fact-checking/media-literacy/2021/should-you-trust-media-bias-charts/

· **Look for Loaded Language**: Language choice is an indicator of bias. Loaded words, such as those with strong connotations (e.g., "government-run" vs. "public"), can manipulate reader perception. It is helpful to compare the same story across different news outlets to identify how language influences perspectives (FAIR). Retrieved from: https://fair.org/take-action-now/media-activism-kit/how-to-detect-bias-in-news-media/

· **Recognize Confirmation Bias**: Understanding and avoiding confirmation bias is crucial. As readers, we often favor content that aligns with our existing beliefs. Being aware of this tendency and actively seeking out differing viewpoints can help mitigate this bias and foster a more balanced understanding (News Literacy Project). Retrieved from: https://newslit.org/tips-tools/understanding-bias/

## 4.9.1 Media Literacy Initiatives

Media literacy is an effective way to help voters recognize bias and seek diverse perspectives:

· **Educational Programs**: Media literacy programs, such as those offered by UNESCO, provide individuals with skills to critically evaluate information, detect misinformation, and understand media's influence on opinions. UNESCO's Media and Information Literacy program aims to educate people on recognizing biases and misinformation and encourages informed media consumption. Retrieved from: https://www.unesco.org/en/media-information-literacy

- **News Literacy Project**: This organization offers tools like infographics and public awareness campaigns that help individuals learn to detect bias in news. It encourages understanding different types of bias and how they manifest in journalism. This initiative helps individuals develop a critical mindset when approaching news media, enabling them to differentiate between facts and slanted narratives (News Literacy Project).

## 4.9.2 The Role of Fact-Checking and Independent Journalism

Fact-checking organizations and independent journalism play a pivotal role in promoting balanced news coverage:

- **Fact-Checking Organizations**: Platforms like FactCheck.org and PolitiFact work independently to verify claims made in the media and political speeches. They play an essential role in holding journalists and politicians accountable, helping consumers access more accurate and objective information.
- **Independent Journalism**: Independent media outlets,

which do not rely on advertising revenue from large corporations, can provide an alternative perspective to mainstream narratives, free from certain pressures that may influence coverage. Initiatives like AllSides provide diverse perspectives by showing the same story covered by multiple outlets with different political biases, encouraging readers to understand various sides of the issue (Poynter).

These strategies, along with media literacy education and the efforts of independent fact-checkers, are essential tools in addressing media bias and empowering consumers to navigate the complex media landscape effectively.

## 4.10 Conclusion

The 2024 U.S. election cycle has underscored the pervasive influence of media bias in shaping voter perceptions and behavior. Media outlets, each with their distinct leanings, have played a critical role in framing the candidates and their policies, often swaying public opinion either positively or negatively. As we have seen throughout the election cycle, the manner in which news is presented, the narratives that are emphasized, and the biases that are embedded in news reporting have collectively influenced voter decisions, shaped political debates, and even affected voter turnout. Media bias, whether subtle or overt, continues to be a force in the democratic process that can either empower or undermine an informed electorate.

In navigating the challenges posed by biased media coverage, media literacy and critical thinking have emerged as vital tools for voters. The ability to critically evaluate the information presented by media outlets, recognize underlying biases, and seek out diverse perspectives is essential for developing a well-rounded understanding of political issues. Initiatives like those promoted by UNESCO and the News Literacy Project emphasize the importance of empowering individuals to identify bias and misinformation and to cultivate informed decision-making skills. In a highly polarized media landscape, the need for media literacy is more urgent than ever to ensure voters can discern fact from opinion, understand the motivations behind news coverage, and make decisions based on balanced and verified information.

As we look ahead, it is clear that media coverage will continue to play a defining role in shaping not only the outcome of the election but also the broader democratic process. The rise of digital and social media has further complicated the media landscape, with algorithms that often reinforce existing biases through echo chambers and filter bubbles. The interplay between media bias, voter behavior, and electoral outcomes is likely to persist as a dynamic and complex issue that warrants attention from policymakers, media organizations, and educators alike. The path forward involves fostering an informed citizenry that can critically engage with the media, hold news outlets accountable, and ultimately strengthen the foundations of democracy through active and informed participation.

2024 has been a powerful reminder of the impact that media can have on shaping public perception, and by extension, the outcomes of democratic processes. Strengthening media literacy and critical thinking among voters is essential in mitigating the negative effects of media bias and ensuring a more equitable and transparent democratic system.

# 5

# Final Thoughts

As we approach the 2024 U.S. elections, the intricate relationship between information manipulation, media bias, and voter perception has never been more apparent. Throughout this book, we have journeyed through the evolution of information manipulation—from its historical roots to its current prominence in shaping political realities today. These dynamics play an undeniable role in influencing how citizens understand the world, form opinions, and ultimately make decisions at the ballot box.

In *Key Terms and Concepts*, we established a foundational understanding of the terminology central to navigating the discussions around media and information manipulation. By defining terms such as "confirmation bias," "echo chambers," "disinformation," and "media framing," readers have been equipped with the tools needed to critically analyze the information they encounter. Understanding these concepts is the first step toward building resilience against manipulative tactics, both intentional and systemic.

In *The Rise of Information Manipulation*, we explored the

growth of modern strategies and tools used to distort information, driven largely by advancements in technology and the prevalence of social media. The proliferation of disinformation campaigns has created an environment where truth is often obscured by sensational narratives, making it increasingly difficult for voters to discern fact from fiction. The implications for democratic processes are profound; as we move closer to the 2024 election, recognizing these tactics becomes crucial to safeguarding electoral integrity.

The *Historical Context of Information Manipulation* chapter provided a broader perspective on how the manipulation of information is not a new phenomenon; rather, it has been a consistent tool of influence for those in power. However, the magnitude and speed at which misinformation spreads today are unprecedented. By understanding historical patterns, we gain insight into the motivations behind these efforts and the resilience required to combat them. History teaches us that while manipulation is an enduring challenge, societal awareness and collective action can diminish its impact.

In *Media Bias and the 2024 US Elections*, we delved into how media outlets, both traditional and digital, contribute to shaping voter behavior. With each outlet presenting information through its own ideological lens, voters are left to navigate a polarized media landscape. As we head into the 2024 elections, media bias has already begun to influence public narratives about candidates, policies, and even the electoral process itself. Bias in media coverage—whether through omission, framing, or selective emphasis—affects not only the candidates who receive visibility but also the public's understanding of critical issues.

The common thread throughout these chapters is the power

of information—how it is wielded, who controls it, and how it impacts the choices we make as a society. The 2024 U.S. elections represent a crucial juncture, with media and information continuing to shape the outcome, the narratives, and, most importantly, voter trust in the democratic process. In such a climate, media literacy and critical thinking become indispensable. Empowering citizens to question the information they consume, understand the biases behind it, and actively seek out diverse perspectives is essential for sustaining a functioning democracy.

As we look toward the future, the way we confront the challenges of information manipulation and media bias will determine the resilience of our democratic institutions. By fostering a culture that values transparency, accountability, and informed participation, we can counteract the forces that seek to divide and manipulate us. The 2024 elections are a pivotal moment—a test of our collective ability to uphold democratic values in the face of evolving threats to truth and free expression. The journey does not end with the election; it is ongoing, and our vigilance and commitment are required every step of the way.

# Reference List

Chapter 1: Key Terms & Concepts


- American Progress. (2019). *Voter Suppression During the 2018 Midterm Elections.* Retrieved from https://www.amer icanprogress.org/article/voter-suppression-2018-midter m-elections/
- Beder, S. (2019). *Public Relations' Role in Manufacturing Artificial Grass Roots Coalitions.* Retrieved from https://ww w.researchgate.net/publication/238304605_Public_Rela tions%E2%80%99_Role_in_Manufacturing_Artificial_ Grass_Roots_Coalitions
- BBC News. (2016). *Pizzagate: The fake story that shows how conspiracy theories spread.* Retrieved from https://www.bbc. com/news/blogs-trending-38156985
- Federal Bureau of Investigation. (2024). *Crime in the United States.* Retrieved from https://www.fbi.gov/how-we-can-

help-you/more-fbi-services-and-information/ucr

- Howard, P. N., & Hussain, M. M. (2013). *Democracy's Fourth Wave? Digital Media and the Arab Spring.* Oxford University Press. Retrieved from https://academic.oup.com/book/122 28/chapter-abstract/161707586?redirectedFrom=fulltext
- New York Times. (2024). *Iran Disinformation Campaign Targets U.S. Presidential Race.* Retrieved from https://www .nytimes.com/2024/09/04/business/media/iran-disinfor mation-us-presidential-race.html
- Search Engine Journal. (2023). *What Are Search Algorithms & How Do They Work?.* Retrieved from https://www.search enginejournal.com/search-engines/algorithms/
- Starbird, K., Maddock, J., Orand, M., Achterman, P., & Mason, R. M. (2014). *Rumors, False Flags, and Digital Vigilantes: Misinformation on X After the 2013 Boston Marathon Bombing.* Retrieved from https://www.researchgate.net/publication /266629432_Rumors_False_Flags_and_Digital_Vigila ntes_Misinformation_on_X_After_the_2013_Boston_ Marathon_Bombing
- Taylor, S., & Johnson, K. (2007). *Until Proven Innocent: Political Correctness and the Shameful Injustices of the Duke Lacrosse Rape Case.* Thomas Dunne Books. Retrieved from https://search.lib.uiowa.edu/primo-explore/fulldisplay/0 1IOWA_ALMA21409559370002771/01IOWA
- Tucker, J. A., Guess, A., Barbera, P., Vaccari, C., Siegel, A., Sanovich, S., Stukal, D., & Nyhan, B. (2018). *Social Media, Political Polarization, and Political Disinformation: A Review of the Scientific Literature.* Retrieved from https://papers.ss rn.com/sol3/papers.cfm?abstract_id=3144139
- Wikipedia. (n.d.). *Malinformation.* Retrieved from https://e n.wikipedia.org/wiki/Malinformation

- World Health Organization (WHO). (2019). *Coronavirus disease (COVID-19) advice for the public: Mythbusters.* Retrieved from https://www.who.int/emergencies/diseases/novel-coronavirus-2019/advice-for-public/myth-busters
- World Health Organization. (2020). *Managing the COVID-19 infodemic: Promoting healthy behaviors and mitigating the harm from misinformation and disinformation.* Retrieved from https://www.who.int/news/item/23-09-2020-managing-the-covid-19-infodemic-promoting-healthy-behaviours-and-mitigating-the-harm-from-misinformation-and-disinformation
- Zuiderveen Borgesius, F. J., Trilling, D., Moeller, J., Bodó, B., de Vreese, C. H., & Helberger, N. (2016). *Should we worry about filter bubbles?* Internet Policy Review, 5(1). Retrieved from https://escholarship.org/content/qt8w7105jp/qt8w7105jp.pdf

Chapter 2: The Rise of Information Manipulation

- CNN. (2024). *Content Creators and Influencers Join DNC to Boost Harris Campaign.* Retrieved from https://edition.cnn.com/2024/08/22/politics/content-creators-influencers-dnc-harris/index.html
- Global Witness. (2024). *U.S. Election: TikTok and Facebook Fail to Block Harmful Disinformation, YouTube Succeeds.* Retrieved from https://www.globalwitness.org/en/campaigns/digital-threats/us-election-tiktok-and-facebook-fail-

block-harmful-disinformation-youtube-succeeds/
- IZEA. (2024). *IZEA Insights: Influencers and the 2024 Election.* Retrieved from https://izea.com/press-releases/izea-insights-influencers-and-the-2024-election/
- Media Matters for America. (2024). *YouTube Has Allowed Conspiracy Theories About Interference in Voting Machines to Go Viral.* Retrieved from https://www.mediamatters.org/google/youtube-has-allowed-conspiracy-theories-about-interference-voting-machines-go-viral
- Menczer, F., & Del Vicario, M. (2021). *Filter Bubbles, Echo Chambers, and Fake News: How Social Media Conditions Individuals to Be Less Critical of Political Misinformation.* Retrieved from https://www.researchgate.net/publication/354459868_Filter_Bubbles_Echo_Chambers_and_Fake_News_How_Social_Media_Conditions_Individuals_to_Be_Less_Critical_of_Political_Misinformation
- News Literacy Project. (n.d.). *Misinformation Dashboard.* Retrieved from https://misinfodashboard.newslit.org/
- Northeastern University. (2024). *Donald Trump Is Relying on Influencers for 2024 Election Campaign.* Retrieved from https://news.northeastern.edu/2024/08/14/donald-trump-influencers/
- Pew Research Center. (2024). *Americans' Views of 2024 Election News.* Retrieved from https://www.pewresearch.org/journalism/2024/10/10/americans-views-of-2024-election-news/
- PMG. (2024). *The Impact of Social Media on the 2024 Presidential Election.* Retrieved from https://www.pmg.com/insights/the-impact-of-social-media-on-the-2024-presidential-election
- Smith, J. D., & Doe, A. (2023). *The Impact of Social Media on*

*Public Health: A Case Study During the COVID-19 Pandemic.* Retrieved from https://pmc.ncbi.nlm.nih.gov/articles/PMC9612566/

- Vicario, M. D., & Menczer, F. (2024). *Election Polls on Social Media: Prevalence, Biases, and Voter Fraud Beliefs.* Retrieved from https://www.researchgate.net/publication/380730958_Election_Polls_on_Social_Media_Prevalence_Biases_and_Voter_Fraud_Beliefs
- YouGov. (2024). *The Role of Disengaged Voters in the 2024 Election: Biden vs. Trump Poll.* Retrieved from https://today.yougov.com/politics/articles/49987-disengaged-voters-role-2024-election-biden-trump-poll

Chapter  4: Media Bias and the 2024 US Elections

- Benson, R. (2017). *Framing Immigrants: News Coverage, Public Opinion, and Policy.* Retrieved from https://www.researchgate.net/publication/316520230_Framing_immigrants_News_coverage_public_opinion_and_policy
- Breitbart. (2024). *'Just Ban It': Donald Trump Vows Executive Action to Keep Men Off Female Sports Teams.* Retrieved from https://www.breitbart.com/politics/2024/10/16/just-ban-it-donald-trump-vows-executive-action-keep-men-off-female-sports-teams/
- CNBC. (2024). *Facebook's Misinformation Problem Has Local Election Officials on Edge.* Retrieved from https://www.cnbc.com/2024/09/26/facebooks-misinformation-problem-

has-local-election-officials-on-edge.html
- Cybersecurity and Infrastructure Security Agency (CISA). (n.d.). *Election Security.* Retrieved from https://www.cisa.gov/topics/election-security
- Daily Caller. (2024). *Environmental Justice Advisors Raked in $500 Million from Taxpayers.* Retrieved from https://dailycaller.com/2024/10/16/environmental-justice-advisors-raked-500-million-taxpayers/
- FAIR. (n.d.). *How to Detect Bias in News Media.* Retrieved from https://fair.org/take-action-now/media-activism-kit/how-to-detect-bias-in-news-media/
- FiveThirtyEight. (n.d.). *Polling Data and Analysis.* Retrieved from https://projects.fivethirtyeight.com/polls/
- Fox News. (2024). *Whistleblowers Claim Border Patrol Surveillance Cameras Are Out of Service; GOP Demands Answers from DHS.* Retrieved from https://www.foxnews.com/us/whistleblowers-border-patrol-surveillance-cameras-out-service-gop-demands-answers-dhs
- News Literacy Project. (n.d.). *Understanding Bias.* Retrieved from https://newslit.org/tips-tools/understanding-bias/
- New York Times. (n.d.). *Voting Rights, Registration, and Requirements.* Retrieved from https://www.nytimes.com/topic/subject/voting-rights-registration-and-requirements
- Pew Research Center. (2024). *Cultural Issues and the 2024 Election.* Retrieved from https://www.pewresearch.org/politics/2024/06/06/cultural-issues-and-the-2024-election/
- Poynter. (2021). *Should You Trust Media Bias Charts?.* Retrieved from https://www.poynter.org/fact-checking/media-literacy/2021/should-you-trust-media-bias-char

ts/

- Reuters Institute for the Study of Journalism. (2024). *Public Perspectives on Trust in News.* Retrieved from https://reutersinstitute.politics.ox.ac.uk/digital-news-report/2024/public-perspectives-trust-news
- SAGE Journals. (2024). *The Dynamics of Political Discourse: Social Media, Misinformation, and Voter Perceptions.* Retrieved from https://journals.sagepub.com/doi/10.1177/13540688231187964
- The Leadership Conference on Civil and Human Rights. (2024). *DOE Voter Registration Toolkit.* Retrieved from https://civilrights.org/2024/02/26/doe-voter-registration-toolkit/
- UNESCO. (n.d.). *Media and Information Literacy.* Retrieved from https://www.unesco.org/en/media-information-literacy
- U.S. Election Assistance Commission (EAC). (n.d.). *Election Security.* Retrieved from https://www.eac.gov/voters/election-security
- Washington Post. (2024). *Economic Inequality and the Rising Tide of Despair: The Case for Redistribution.* Retrieved from https://www.washingtonpost.com/opinions/2024/01/25/economic-inequality-despair-redistribution/